"I love this book! It is exactly what today's moms need to tackle the real issues we face. Marina and Gregory help us apply biblical wisdom to specific, real-life situations. An excellent, timely book. Highly needed and strongly recommended."

— Dr. Leslie Parrott, author of *You Matter More Than You Think*

Praise for *Be the Best Mom You Can Be*

"Marina and Gregory Slayton have written a great book for moms. *Be the Best Mom You Can Be* will help mothers of all types to raise up their families in healthy and positive ways despite all the craziness in the world around us. I heartily recommend this book for moms and even for dads who want to help their wives to be the best moms they can be."

— Eric Metaxas, *New York Times* best-selling author of *Miracles* and *Bonhoeffer*

"The challenges facing today's families are substantial. We moms must face those challenges head on with wisdom, love, and joy. Marina and Gregory Slayton bring more than twenty-five years of wisdom, love, and joy to this great book, which will be a blessing to every mom who reads it. Building on Gregory's international bestseller *Be a Better Dad Today*, *Be the Best Mom You Can Be* is a wonderful book for all of us twenty-first century moms."

— US Senator Kelly Ayotte (R-NH)

"My dear friends Marina and Gregory Slayton have written an international bestseller for dads; *Be a Better Dad Today* has sold more than 150,000 copies worldwide in just three years. But this next book for moms may be even better. Written primarily by Marina who has both researched the subject carefully and has more than twenty-five years as a mother of four great kids, this is a wonderful book for all moms who are looking for the wisdom, the faith, and the strength they need to be the best moms they can be.

This is a beautiful book written from the heart, showing moms how a life lived in Christ can heal and transform all that goes before it. This book will help moms and dads to raise stronger, wiser, and more virtuous children. I highly recommend this great work."

— Fr. Jonathan Kalisch, OP Priest in Residence, Saint John Paul II National Shrine, Washington, DC

BE THE BEST MOM YOU CAN BE

A Practical Guide to Raising Whole Children in a Broken Generation

Marina Slayton
and Gregory W. Slayton

NELSON
BOOKS

An Imprint of Thomas Nelson

Published in Nashville, Tennessee, by Nelson Books, an imprint of Thomas Nelson. Nelson Books and Thomas Nelson are registered trademarks of HarperCollins Christian Publishing, Inc.

Authors are represented by the literary agents Jay Mitchell, 8S Dooley Avenue, First Floor, Richmond, Virginia, and Bill Dallas, PO Box 371015, Montara, California.

Thomas Nelson, Inc., titles may be purchased in bulk for educational, business, fund-raising, or sales promotional use. For information, please e-mail SpecialMarkets@ThomasNelson.com.

Unless otherwise marked, Scripture quotations are taken from the Holy Bible, New International Version®, NIV®. Copyright © 1973, 1978, 1984, 2011 by Biblica, Inc.™ Used by permission of Zondervan. All rights reserved worldwide. www.zondervan.com

Scripture quotations marked NKJV are taken from THE NEW KING JAMES VERSION. © 1982 by Thomas Nelson, Inc. Used by permission. All rights reserved.

Scripture quotations marked ESV are taken from THE ENGLISH STANDARD VERSION. © 2001 by Crossway Bibles, a division of Good News Publishers.

Scripture quotations marked MSG are taken from The Message by Eugene H. Peterson. © 1993, 1994, 1995, 1996, 2000. Used by permission of NavPress Publishing Group. All rights reserved.

Scripture quotations marked NASB are taken from NEW AMERICAN STANDARD BIBLE®, © The Lockman Foundation 1960, 1962, 1963, 1968, 1971, 1972, 1973, 1975, 1977, 1995. Used by permission.

Scripture quotations marked KJV are taken from the King James Version of the Bible. Public domain.

Some names and identifying details have been changed in this book to protect the privacy of the individuals involved.

Library of Congress Cataloging-in-Publication Data

Slayton, Marina, 1960– author.
  Be the best mom you can be : a practical guide to raising whole children in a broken generation / Marina and Gregory W. Slayton, Marina and Gregory W. Slayton.
    pages cm
  ISBN 978-0-7180-2214-3 (hardback)
  1. Mother and child—Religious aspects—Christianity. 2. Child rearing—Religious aspects—Christianity. I. Slayton, Gregory, author. II. Title.
  BV4529.18.S59 2015
  248.8'431—dc23   2014032496

Printed in the United States of America

15 16 17 18 19 RRD 6 5 4 3 2 1

For Gregory, Sasha, Christian, Daniel,
and Nicholas . . . always

Contents

Foreword

by Cathy McMorris Rodgers

I love being a wife and mother. I also love the honor of serving as an elected official; it is a great joy and a true privilege.
And being a senior member of House leadership is something
I never dreamed of happening to me. I know in my heart that
both those public roles will eventually come to an end, but my
role as mother in my loving and caring family will never come
to an end. It is my greatest joy, my most important role, and the
greatest gift that God has given to me.

But these days it is tougher and tougher for moms and dads
to build strong and loving families. We live in difficult times, in a
broken culture. Many of us come from fractured homes. The path
to happy families is not easy to find. That's why I love this book.

Today too many moms feel stressed and inadequate facing
the challenges of motherhood in the twenty-first century. We
can be so overwhelmed by juggling the "tyranny of the trivial"—
work in or out of the house, meals, cleaning, bills, carpooling,

soccer practices, SATs, shopping, renovations, homework, and so much more—that we can forget to build a family on the foundations of love and faith.

The sad reality is that in today's society motherhood is much less valued than it was just two generations ago. These challenges can quickly drown out what is most important: nurturing, enjoying, and building our families. For many of us the biggest question is how to remain joyful in the face of these challenges. How do we remain focused on what is truly important in our lives and the lives of our families? And how do we build our families to be bastions of love, wisdom, and strength for all family members? This book helps us moms do just that.

All moms need help to be the best mothers they can be. Marina Slayton, along with her husband Gregory, has written that kind of book. *Be the Best Mom You Can Be* is a truly helpful, deeply practical book for moms everywhere. Many years of research and more than twenty-five years of parenting four wonderful children have inspired this book. Through reading it, we moms will be better equipped to handle the great challenges we all face.

Marina learned how to be a good mom without her own mom's help. This is the case for many who learn how to be good moms without good examples. This inspirational and highly personal book is a resource for us as we help our families navigate through the brokenness around us. The outside world pushes onto us questions of sex, drugs, and societal expectations. Inside, we must fight insecurity and even our own aspirations for our children. Marina speaks to these challenges in a clear, step-by-step fashion.

The greatest gift we can give our children is a sense of

belonging, a place in the family and from there a place in the world. Marina and Gregory provide clear wisdom in how to build this wholeness from the brokenness surrounding us. They have raised their kids not to be overwhelmed by the challenges all around us. This book will help all us moms to raise our children with wisdom, joy, and love. I thank my friends Gregory and Marina for writing this book. And I hope it will be a true blessing to you and yours as it has been to ours.

—The Honorable C. M. R.

Introduction

If you are like most moms (including me!) you probably feel stress and insecurity facing the challenges of being a mom in the twenty-first century. We want to raise kids who will go on to live loving, productive lives. And we would like to feel content and hopeful while we build into our families. But our desires are often complicated by busy lives, little or no support from our extended families, and our increasingly dysfunctional culture.

Wherever you are in your life, there is no person or family beyond God's ability to redeem. If there were, I would not be writing these words. I could be dead because my mother took drugs to abort me. I could be divorced because I bailed out on all my relationships before Gregory. I could have a terrible relationship with my four children because of my own upbringing. The fact that none of these has happened is proof of the redeeming power of Jesus—not because I have the ability to create life from death. None of us does.

Instead of feeling stressed and insecure about our families, God has created us to be hopeful, joyful, and peaceful as moms. So how do we face the challenges of modern-day motherhood with joy, hope, and peace? How do we raise our kids not to break in the face of the brokenness around us? I have wrestled with these questions for more than twenty-five years.

Moms matter. What we do will be remembered long after we are gone. Our lives are our greatest legacy to our children and their children's children. The world wants to label us and establish our identity by using those labels. But God wants us to know and be confident of our identity in Him. God knows each and every one of us by name. We are not alone in our motherhood journey. Jesus is with us each and every step of the way.

The intent of this book is to help us build our families on His strong foundations of faith, wisdom, and love. There are no pony tricks to being a good mom, no "one-size-fits-all" rules that work for every family. This reality makes it imperative for moms to process our specific situations in life by asking the right questions and seeking meaningful answers. By highlighting the most pressing questions facing moms today, I want to help you discern how you can raise your kids well in a broken world. We cannot shy away from these issues because the world does not shy away from them. At the end of each chapter, I have designed a series of purposeful questions in order to help you process your unique situation wisely. With wisdom and grace we can raise whole kids even in our broken culture—all while living in hope, joy, and peace.

ELUSIVE PERFECTION

I was raised by a broken mother, but I did not become a broken mom to my children. Perfection has eluded me, but love has not. Gregory and I have four children, ages twenty-five to fourteen. Like most families, we have lived through the best of times and the worst of times. I would count this season of my life as inhabiting both those realities. In 2012 my husband and I traveled to China on business, and I came down with a devastating virus that has not left my system. While battling exhaustion caused by the virus, I've also had to deal with what my physician says is permanent facial nerve damage. I usually brush my teeth with my back to the mirror so I don't feel discouraged at the beginning of the day. The love that Gregory and our four children—Sasha, Christian, Daniel, and Nicholas—have shown me through this challenging season is a tangible reflection that God is love no matter our circumstances, no matter our brokenness.

I am convinced that today, more than ever, moms require deep wisdom to deal with the brokenness all around us and within us. I discovered that I would have to seek healing for my own brokenness so I could raise children who are capable of leading whole lives. We all desire to be moms who thrive and not just survive. And we want the same for our children. We do this by acquiring both wholeness and wisdom so we are victors instead of victims. Our heavenly Father lovingly provides this healing wisdom over time to all who are willing to hear Him.

Motherhood is a humbling journey. Through being moms (and wives—but that is discussion for a different book) we learn about ourselves and who we truly are—and not how we hope the outside world sees us. We cannot hide from our true selves among our family members. Frankly, it has been in my family life that I discovered all the areas of my life that need God's healing touch. Being a single, professional woman through most of my twenties meant I focused mostly on developing my life. Not a bad thing, but I simply did not understand the process of the "iron sharpening iron" metaphor until I married. It has been in partnership with my wonderful husband and terrific kids that who I am at my very core has been revealed to me.

I thought I would take to motherhood as a duck takes to water, so the challenges that naturally come with motherhood were somewhat of a shock to me. I guess I thought it would be about baking cookies, reading books, and going on picnics and trips. Everything I love with everyone I love. But the reality of motherhood is that it brings all of a mom's experiences and feelings to the fore, and if those experiences and feelings have been wounded, inner healing becomes mandatory if we don't want to repeat going down that same path of hurt and pain.

It is God's desire to bring wholeness not only to us as moms but also to our children. Wholeness arising from brokenness is the story of many moms I know, and it is my own story. I had to learn how to be an emotionally and spiritually healthy mom to my children. I have worked hard to equip my kids with the wisdom and discernment to stand up to the tough moral and ethical situations that all our children now face in our twenty-first-century culture.

Mothers require courage, wisdom, and spiritual armor (Eph. 6:10–17). Even if our families are whole, we have to deal with the extensive spiritual and emotional brokenness of this day and age. The cultural pressures our children face and the foolishness they see all around them are far beyond anything most of us experienced in our own youth. We must help our children deal with this cultural tsunami. We must prepare them to deal with the rising trend in our culture of calling foolish or even dangerous behavior wise or appropriate. Moms have the full resource and spiritual armor of God as we build into our families. Truth, righteousness, the gospel of peace, faith, salvation, and the sword of the Spirit have all been made available to us to counteract the prevailing cultural winds.

PARENTAL INSECURITY

Like many in our generation, I have experienced deep insecurity in my "performance" as a mom. Parental anxiety is an ever-present reality for many moms, and it is leading many to become so-called helicopter parents. These moms hover over and protect their children to such an extent that the children frequently grow up to be helpless and narcissistic. We have to ask what our insecurity is doing to our children.

Many moms are anxious, and their children, in turn, are filled with anxiety. Our own ambitions and the fear of not measuring up to impossible societal standards are feeding this anxiety. The tendency to focus on ourselves to the detriment of our families and communities has been percolating for decades. It arises because we desire worldly accomplishments above all else; this is how our society validates us as good moms. Therefore we are raising our kids to want to be famous, to have a lot of material goods, and to be the envy of their generation. This is the opposite of what God wants for our kids. Our heavenly Father wants our children to be people of character, competence, and commitment. Proverbs 16:16 instructs us that wisdom is to be desired above gold—that is to say, your character (who you are) is more important than worldly success (what you do). Yes, we all want kids who succeed in life, but ultimately we have to surrender our definition of *success* to the Lord. Our legacy to our children must focus on helping them develop wisdom and wholeness so that they can deal with the pain, the joy, and the messiness of life.

In the Old Testament there is a saying in Ezekiel 16:44: "Like mother, like daughter." It is imperative for us moms to work through our own personal issues, not only for ourselves but also for our spouses and children. We don't want our kids to fall into broken behavior, so it is imperative that we are honest about our own brokenness and the brokenness of our culture and that we equip ourselves with the wisdom to effectively deal with these issues.

INSPIRATION FOR MOMS

Every day I ask our heavenly Father to help me love my family, to give me the wisdom to be a good mom, and to fill my heart with prayer. Family life can be challenging because we are dealing with the realities of human nature, both our own and our family members'. There are days, and even entire seasons, when I struggle to be the best mom I can be. No matter the circumstances or my mood, through seeking God in His Word and in prayer I try to put myself in a position where the Holy Spirit can encourage me and inspire me to press on. And that can make all the difference.

Through faith, I have come to believe that the Bible holds the wisdom we need to raise wise, virtuous children in a fractured generation. God can truly speak to us through His Word. Careful, daily study of the Bible has supported me through some of the most challenging seasons of life. I have learned that we as moms can greatly benefit from the apostle Paul's exhortation to "pray without ceasing" (1 Thess. 5:17 NKJV). Prayer is the single greatest spiritual weapon we have as mothers. Continual prayer helps us deal not only with the challenges of our children but also with our own angst, wondering, *Am I doing this right?* To help us grow in the area of prayer, we will look much more at the power and purpose of prayer in the final chapter.

There are no quick tricks to mothering; there is only a daily resolution to commit yourself to the Lord and to your family, always asking for His grace. Our commitment to unconditional love is the basis of all good mothering. We all long for life's difficulties to be wrapped up in a pretty bow at the end; we all want to experience closure in our lives. But life is not a romantic novel, nor is it an hour-long television drama. On this side of heaven we will not always have the benefit of a happy ending. Yet children who witness their mom (and hopefully their dad) practicing biblical wisdom will be able to embrace life in all its complexity and grow to a mature understanding of reality—two of the greatest gifts we can give our kids.

GENERATIONAL BROKENNESS

I was born in New York City. My father, Sergei, was born in St. Petersburg in 1913 as part of the intelligentsia, the highly educated class of prerevolutionary Russia. He was an older man by the time my brother, Alex, and I were born. We called him Papa. My Polish-born mother, a much younger woman, had the unusual name of Bozena. She also came from an aristocratic background, and like my father, she was a victim of the turbulent and terrible events of the twentieth century. Separately they sought sanctuary on the shores of the United States as refugees from World War II Europe and the advent of Communism. They both came through Ellis Island and met in New York City. They were married in Manhattan in 1956.

Like many middle-class parents, my parents moved to the suburbs of New Jersey because they were unable to afford private schools for my brother and me in New York City. They commuted into the city for their jobs. My mom had defected from Communist Poland without receiving her university degree, so she cobbled a career in fashion that gave her both a commission and a pension. While she enjoyed fashion, she did not earn much. Her experience made her determined that I would have professional skills that would not leave me dependent on a husband for finances. My father had been a lawyer in Europe but became a structural engineer in New York because he lacked proficient English to pursue law in America. I think he was wistful of what might have been, but in the wake of the destruction of World War II he was grateful to start fresh in America and establish a stable foundation for his children. My parents labored without complaint to pay the mortgage and the hospital bills for my sick grandmother until she passed away. Ours was a fairly typical immigrant story.

My parents survived the horrors of war and did not emerge from those traumas unscathed. Their experiences did not lead them to faith; they could best be described as agnostic. At the same time, my parents used religion as one way of maintaining their disparate cultural traditions. I was raised as a Roman

Catholic, following my mother's tradition. I remember the pretty white lace dress and the beautiful gold cross I received for communion. My father was Russian Orthodox, so my brother was confirmed in that tradition. We did not consistently go to either church as we grew up.

My mother was a wonderful hostess, one of the most charming I have ever known. Both of my parents were talented linguists; my mother spoke four languages and my father had command of six. They came from similar cultures that highly valued education and cultural pursuits. Even though they shared much in common, including tremendous personal suffering, my parents had a destructive marriage.

My mom grew up with a gambling father whose spendthrift ways forced her mother to pawn jewelry to buy milk for her. Stranded without money, my grandmother sent a telegram to her father for train fare home. My great-grandfather, a nobleman with a large estate outside Cracow, Poland, had pleaded with my grandmother not to marry the wastrel. But in a scene worthy of a Russian novel, my grandfather-to-be had whipped out a pistol and threatened to commit suicide if my beautiful grandmother did not consent to marriage. My gentle grandmother gave in, and the disaster prophesied by her father indeed came to pass. Deeply humbled, my grandmother returned with my mom to her family's estate—only to see her father die of pneumonia six months later.

My grandmother and my mother witnessed the catastrophic events of World War II from the city of Warsaw. My mom even participated in the Warsaw Uprising of 1944 as a teenage courier. As a result, they were marched off by the Nazis to concentration camps prepared for the Polish Underground Army. These camps were adjacent to Auschwitz. Mom went through unimaginable horrors that broke her spirit in many ways.

My father was abandoned by his parents to an orphanage during the Russian Revolution. There he experienced things no child should. He ran in packs of children who hunted for cats and dogs to eat. He eventually rejoined his parents in Poland, where they had settled, only to live through World War II. My father lived in seven different countries before making his way to Ellis Island. Once there he had to start from scratch yet again.

My father eventually recovered because he knew how to forgive. My mother, on the other hand, never forgave. Her lack of forgiveness eventually destroyed her. She became an alcoholic, an adulteress, and an addict of tranquilizers. She simply could not overcome the traumas of her past. She did not know how to be a stable mom because she lacked any stability herself. But my mother did understand, thankfully, that family is essential and that sacrifice is part of life. So I was handed a mixed bag in terms of role models. Because of my parents' strong cultural traditions, I understood that building a family requires nurturing, support, and sacrifice. I knew that families are not built on dreams but through daily hard work. But I didn't understand how to build a happy and harmonious family because I did not have that experience growing up.

Being raised in a home filled with bitterness was deeply painful. My father retreated into the den to sleep and do his own thing. My mom threatened divorce with sad regularity. When I was twelve she told me that she had taken drugs to induce an abortion while she was carrying me. This was one of many deeply scarring memories I still carry from my childhood.

As a result, I carried deep emotional wounds into my teenage years—wounds that I had no way to deal with. I became anorexic before anyone understood what it meant. I had quite a few boyfriends, always looking for love. I turned to school for validation and did well academically. I saved my money and traveled whenever I could; in fact, the happiest times I had with my parents were spent traveling, enjoying different cultures, expanding my knowledge of history, and eating terrific food. Not coincidentally, I now travel with my husband and children all the time, replicating the happiest moments of my childhood.

BECOMING A BELIEVER

I was not a Christian when I entered Amherst College, but I left a believer. These were the years when I was asking big philosophical questions about life, unencumbered by material concerns. This was also the late 1970s when feminism was in full swing. My female classmates were diverse and energetic. I enjoyed being around passionate women who were also asking big questions. They were committed to a cause beyond themselves.

Eventually I found the answers to my questions not in philosophy or religion but in a relationship with Jesus Christ. I was particularly influenced by a woman at college who was blind and suffered from rheumatoid arthritis. Her patience and peace in the face of suffering was inspiring. Her example stirred a desire in me to pursue a spiritual line of inquiry. I wanted to experience the same joy my friend had through various Bible studies on campus and spiritual retreats. Through her example and that of other dear friends whom I deeply respected, I became a Christian.

After graduating from Amherst College, I went to Columbia University where I received two master's degrees. I went on to teach college-level English. After several years working in New York, I ended up in Boston running an adult literacy center and sitting on the Massachusetts Governor's Task Force for the Working Poor. I began to specialize in adult literacy, a work I found rewarding. Like the rest of my generation, I was pulled and pushed by the rapidly changing morality of our times. However, one great truth I realized early on: I believe in a relationship and not a religion. I have a personal relationship with Jesus. Without His help, I could not have survived, let alone thrived, in my life.

MARRIAGE AND FAMILY

I married my husband, Gregory, in 1989. We had been good friends since college. We met through an intercollegiate faith group while I was at Amherst College and he was at Dartmouth College. Gregory is a dynamic husband and father. Our three older children are beginning their adult lives. The oldest two have graduated from Ivy League schools, and our third is at SMU in Dallas. Our eldest daughter is a lieutenant in the US Army in South Korea. Our youngest son is a joy. I marvel that my husband and I have been able to build such a loving family life. We see this as a miraculous answer to prayer and a product of faith. The brokenness in my own life, and in my husband's life, has become an opportunity for grace and redemption.

Gregory is passionate about being a husband and father, and he is committed to mentoring the next generation through the ministry of fatherhood, family, and faith. He wrote the international bestseller *Be a Better Dad Today: Ten Tools Every Father*

Needs[1] because we believe that families are worth fighting for. We cannot take the incredibly important ministry for granted, for it is written that before the great day of the Lord "He will turn the hearts of the parents to their children, and the hearts of the children to their parents" (Mal. 4:6).

All of us go through struggles in life. But as Christians, we can be confident that Jesus Himself will be walking with us, guiding and loving us. In Christ we can trust that the end will be good, wherever we are on the journey today. Whether you are on your first step or near your last, we are created to walk with purpose and passion. With Christ's help on the journey, we can become moms who have the wisdom to help our kids thrive despite the pervasive brokenness of this generation.

FOR FURTHER REFLECTION

Ponder

God's Word

[To] all who mourn . . .
[he will] bestow on them a crown of beauty instead of ashes,
the oil of joy instead of mourning,
and a garment of praise instead of a spirit of despair.
They will be called oaks of righteousness,
a planting of the LORD for the display of his splendor.
    (Isa. 61:2–3)

Not that I have already obtained all this, or have already arrived at my goal, but I press on to take hold of that for which Christ Jesus took hold of me. Brothers and sisters, I do not consider myself yet to have taken hold of it. But one thing I do: Forgetting what is behind and straining toward what is ahead, I press on toward the goal to win the prize for which God has called me heavenward in Christ Jesus. (Phil. 3:12–14)

Charm is deceptive, and beauty is fleeting;
but a woman who fears the LORD is to be praised.
    (Prov. 31:30)

The Authors' Words
"Perfection has eluded me, but love has not."

Assess

Honestly reflect on your own journey as a girl, a woman, and now a mother. Assess your own strengths and weaknesses in light of the Scriptures.

1. What do you want, both for yourself and your family?
2. What hindrances do you need to leave behind from your childhood?
3. What have you achieved thus far in your life?
4. In what ways do you feel that you are in a conversation with God?
5. What specific goals are you pressing on toward?
6. Have you taken the time to write your life story? How does your life story so far impact you as a wife and mother today?

Sum Up

Our legacy to our children will impact generations to come. Moms require the wisdom to raise kids who have character and a strong moral center. We begin this process by being confident of our identity in Christ and knowing that our lives have purpose and meaning.

One

A Wise Mom: Love Is the Foundation

Why start with love? Because we know that our children are growing up in a world that is increasingly devoid of affirming, life-giving love. After more than thirty-five years of walking in faith, I appreciate ever more deeply how profoundly rich are the tenets of our faith. We need to draw from these bedrock truths as we confront the challenges facing families today. Let us begin by reminding ourselves what the apostle John wrote to a mother almost two thousand years ago: "I am not writing you a new command but one we have had from the beginning. I ask that we love one another. And this is love: that we walk in obedience to his commands. As you have heard from the beginning, his command is that you walk in love" (2 John 1:5–6). How wonderful it is to be ministers of love to our children, just as He ministers to us in love. The more I go on in faith, the more I realize the beautiful simplicity of our walk with Jesus.

However, there is a crisis of love in this generation. We all recognize what has become a sadly pervasive truth: many parents don't feel love themselves and many families today are not able to show their own kids the love and guidance they so desperately need. As Leo Tolstoy wrote in his famous opening line in *Anna Karenina*: "All happy families are alike, each unhappy family is unhappy in its own way." This holds true today: love is the basis of every happy family. Obviously, expressions of love run the gamut, but in a happy family each family member knows that through the dramas and joys of life, he or she is loved.

My mom saw her life in the context of her own pain and suffering. A survivor of World War II and German concentration camps, she carried even deeper emotional wounds of rejection from when her father abandoned her mother and herself for a life of amusement and pleasure. My husband's family background was similarly complicated.

The Lord, in bringing Gregory and me together, demonstrated that He is more than able to build strong families even when we carry heavy burdens of family brokenness. We are examples that our heavenly Father can make families and marriages whole no matter what. God took a real risk in bringing the two of us together. On paper, we seemed a perfect match, with similar educational backgrounds. But internally we are both extremely sensitive to rejection and hurt. The fact that the Lord has worked in us to create a strong and happy family is a testimony to the fact that He is able to redeem anyone.

God's call to us is this: *Let Me minister to you My love.* This is where we find wholeness and peace. Stop looking to the world for validation because ultimately it is transitory and dissatisfying. The Lord taught me that we can all be freed from past broken behavior. We can gain the strength to create healthy, happy families. We do not have to cave into the cultural pressures of our age. We do not have to fear making a decision because we are not sure of what to do next. Our journey begins by looking to God to guide us to the healing answers that give our lives meaning, love, and belonging. These, in turn, give us purpose and vision.

LOVE AS THE FOUNDATION

Before I became a Christian, I used the word *love* to justify relationships that were not healthy. I looked for love in places I should not, and I see now that I was looking for ways to satisfy the emptiness in me. I wanted to move from the ordinary to the extraordinary, and love gave me a feeling of transcendence that I so desired in a temporal world. And because I had not felt loved and protected in my childhood, I searched for love and made it my idol. I did not even understand what I meant by love because of my brokenness.

In my relationships prior to my marriage, I kept looking for validation through love. I eventually realized that while love may feel like sweetness and light at the start, over time it becomes a matter of discipline in the face of the difficult and the mundane. Like many in our culture, I idolized love in a dangerous way. I aspired to a Hollywood-type romantic love, not realizing the unrealistic promises of this media-inspired goal. Worshipping love is a cruel taskmaster because love becomes disposable when it no longer satisfies. I wanted a dream, but every time I entered a relationship I ended up with a human being.

This is not the biblical understanding of love at all. Before Gregory, none of my romantic relationships could withstand the impact of reality. Fortunately God showed me compassion, and through the work of the Holy Spirit I learned to practice love even when my feelings were not falling into line. True love, I came to realize, has to be tied to a worldview higher than myself. It must be cultivated and outwardly practiced so that it survives even when immediate satisfaction is not evident. I also realized that my heart was not the unending source of love I needed it to be. It became clear that I required a source for the love I could not supply from within.

Just as with a lack of oxygen, we cannot survive without love. But oxygen has a source, as does love. Do you have a source of love that you can go to and draw from on a regular basis? Moms have at the ready an eternal and unlimited source of love that we can draw on whenever we need more in our own lives. This love in turn can flow to those who depend on us. This is where our faith as Christians is so valuable. Ultimately we can love others because He first loved us (1 John 4:19). Do you know that you are loved and cherished? The strength and knowledge that this brings will give us the ability to weather the struggles of mothering. When I glimpsed the depth of Jesus' love for me, my brokenness was shattered and He could begin the redeeming healing so necessary in my life. His love supplies and feeds my great love for my family.

LOVE AS REDEEMER

As moms, love is something that is in our power to give, and it is what our children yearn for every day. The single greatest gift that you give your children is to love them; they will continuously draw from this well as they grow and mature. If you poison this well with anger, bitterness, manipulation, or any number of toxins arising from your own brokenness, you will only perpetuate that same brokenness in their lives. But our God is the Redeemer whose heart is to save and heal all those who come to Him.

Our heavenly Father wants His people to experience redemption through healing and wholeness. That is possible for us all because of His love.

The basis of the Christian faith is that "God is love" (1 John 4:8). Man and woman in the Garden of Eden were expressions of His love. But through disobedience, humanity went into exile from the loving and holy presence of God. Sin cannot exist in the presence of a holy God. We cannot relate to God on our own terms. Ultimately, it is only through the loving atonement of His Son, Jesus Christ, who bore our transgressions on the Cross at Calvary, that we can be reconciled to our eternal Father and brought into His eternal family: "For God so loved the world that he gave his one and only Son, that whoever believes in him shall not perish but have eternal life" (John 3:16).

I had no problems recognizing I was a sinner. I know some struggle over the issue of sin but perhaps being raised by perfectionist parents ironically served a higher purpose in my life. What I could not envision was how to get from who I was to who I wanted to be. But God could, and He has done a great work in me and in my family. He can do that for you as well.

Whether you are in a family filled with faith, or quite the opposite, it is essential that you practice the discipline of love. A mom gets up at night to feed a crying baby, brushes her child's teeth before her own, spends years being a taxi driver (without tips), and becomes an academic tutor for decades. A wife and mom must take care of the home, cultivate her relationship with her husband, and then work on her own life. That's the core of motherhood: sacrificial love. It is beautiful and powerful. But it is not easy.

A WELL OF FORGIVENESS

Love is an invaluable source of forgiveness: "Love covers over a multitude of sins" (1 Pet. 4:8). Our love for our families is a well of forgiveness. We are called to forgive regardless, but if we cultivate love we will forgive with freedom. Loving fully means that we give our children the sense of belonging and security they crave no matter their response. Love takes the shortcomings of others and releases God's power within us to forgive and even to bless. Love is the bedrock of all happy families.

Gloriously, Jesus tells us that our heavenly Father is Love. This is hard to fully fathom, but it's not just that our Father loves us; He is Love. All of us who need a fresh touch of love can meditate on the truth that our God is Love. So if you need more love in your life, ask Him to give you more. He appreciates it when His children ask for good gifts to be used to bless others.

What happens when we as parents choose not to follow the challenging but eternally rewarding path of love? The following poignant story will serve to illustrate the destruction that comes to a family that allows selfish tendencies to supplant sacrifice and love.

Our daughter attended a very competitive private school. Every year this school sent an incredible number of its students to all the best colleges. Yet my husband and I found that for all the great academics, the prevailing atmosphere of materialistic consumption was difficult to deal with. As parents we tried hard to help our kids understand that life is not about having things but about faith.

Extreme affluence, however, was not the most challenging aspect of life in this school; rather, it was the rampant self-centeredness of many busy parents that led them to effectively abandon their kids. This is especially painful for teenagers, as they are highly unlikely to make a fuss or ask directly for help. That makes it easy for overly busy parents to emotionally abandon their teens. But parents are very much needed in the challenging teen years. It was so sad to see bright and talented ten-year-olds become surly, seen-it-all, dispirited sixteen-year-olds. Drug abuse and depression, even suicides, were far too common.

Kyra was my daughter Sasha's best friend from grades six through eight. Kyra entered sixth grade with a cheerful demeanor and beautiful long blonde hair. Her father was rarely around, but her mother was a stunning woman who seemed to have a perpetual smile. After several years in Palo Alto, we moved back to the East Coast in order to reverse certain negative patterns we had noted in our daughter. As we will discuss later in the book, changing your family's setting and subculture can be a wise parental strategy if your children are being overwhelmed by a negative or self-destructive situation.

In any event, Sasha was very lonely at our new home in Virginia, and she wanted to invite Kyra to visit for Christmas. We acceded to her wishes, confident that no mom would allow her only daughter of fourteen to be away for all of the Christmas holiday. Imagine our surprise when I spoke with Kyra's mom and found she was not only willing but enthusiastic about Kyra coming to stay with us for the entire Christmas holiday. Kyra stepped off the plane having chopped off her glorious butter-colored hair and dyed it black. Kyra suddenly appeared hard and much older.

It was not a successful visit because Sasha, under the influence of her sad and angry friend, grew whiny and bitter. I am ashamed to say it, but I was relieved when Kyra flew home. Several months later Sasha came into our kitchen crying. Kyra's parents had called a family meeting. They sat Kyra and her older brother on the sofa and said, "Kids, we have a problem. We are getting a divorce and neither one of us wants to take either one of you." Gregory and I had long sensed all was not right in Kyra's family but their blatant disregard of the kids' needs and feelings shocked us to the core. We could only imagine the devastating impact it must have had on Kyra and her brother.

Sasha wanted to know if we could take Kyra. Of course we said yes, but we felt real internal tension. While we wanted to be loving and kind to our daughter's friend, we also wanted to be wise for our entire family. Ultimately we were responsible for Sasha and her brothers first and foremost. We believe 1 Corinthians 15:33: "Do not be misled: 'Bad company corrupts good character.'" Kyra's negative influence on my daughter was sadly evident, and we would not be able to protect Sasha if Kyra lived with us. But how could we reject a rejected child?

Ultimately, Kyra went to live with her grandmother. Today she is knocking around various cities, never having finished college, still looking for a place to belong.

Every child wants to know that he or she belongs. The root in *belongs* is *longs*; every child longs to be at the center of his or her mom's and dad's hearts. This is key to every child. But Kyra, like many children today, was not given a sense of belonging.

Instead, she was given a sense of rejection. This is a burden that no human being should have to bear.

We did take active steps to respond to Sasha's sense of isolation in Virginia. We developed a riding program through a local show barn. Sasha started to take weekly singing lessons with a fabulous teacher. Most importantly, Sasha and I spent a lot of time together. We shopped in old-town Alexandria, went to wonderful restaurants, and took long walks together. I had quite a bit to do that year: relocate our family of six, finish a major renovation in our new home, and then organize our family's move to Bermuda. All this with a three-year-old joined at the hip. But it was a joy to be my daughter's best friend that year—when she needed it most.

FOCUSING ON LOVE

Love kept me focused on the most important element of our lives: our family. As moms, we must never forget that our kids are given to us for a finite period of time. While we can, we need to nurture and love them as much as possible. In doing so, we give our children the gift of knowing they are truly and richly loved. The days of childhood will come to an end before we know it.

There is no substitute for time; we all know this. But the tyranny of the trivial can drown out what we most need to do. It is not easy, but it is necessary to sacrifice the busy for the important. I have needed lots of discernment in this area of life, but I have never regretted that I gave up many personal pursuits for an extended period of my life. This has been for the greater good of my family. Now that my children no longer require the same level of custodial care, my life is establishing an entirely different rhythm.

Children are born with an innate ability to look for love in the right place: their parents. But if we reject our own children, what will they do as teens and adults? They will seek love in all the wrong places. Kids are not fooled. They can discern when the people who are supposed to love them most do not.

Second Timothy 3:1–2 reflects the prevailing culture in America: "But understand this, that in the last days there will come times of difficulty. For people will be lovers of self" (ESV). Parents who cannot keep their own selfish interests in check make family life very painful. Sadly, my family saw this same pattern repeated multiple times in Silicon Valley, in Bermuda, and in Hanover, New Hampshire, where our middle son went to a well-regarded and competitive high school. The rising tide of parental neglect and abandonment contributed to suicides and attempted suicides in all three localities.

In the early 1990s, I cofounded with Rebecca White the first Mothers' Group for Redeemer Presbyterian in New York City. Rebecca and I were enthusiastic young moms with very young children. We decided to bring together like-minded young moms in order to build community in highly fragmented Manhattan. Besides holding weekly meetings, we hosted monthly talks given by respected, experienced moms with older children. These talks provided our group with much needed advice and counsel. Kathy Keller, the wife of Tim Keller, the head pastor of Redeemer, graciously came to speak to us one Tuesday morning in May. Kathy and Tim actually lived a few floors above us in our apartment building on Roosevelt Island—a divine coincidence for Gregory and me in many ways.

As we drove from our apartment building to the Upper West Side church where our group met, Kathy and I got into an interesting conversation about children. Kathy has three sons and is deeply committed to her family. At the time, my daughter Sasha was only six months old and I was quite an anxious mother. Kathy mentioned that Tim still mentored doctoral students at Westminster Theological Seminary in Philadelphia. Tim was working with one PhD student who wanted to answer the critical question of why children of Christian parents choose to embrace or reject Christianity as adults. After years of research, the doctoral student came to the conclusion that there was one overwhelming factor in why children decide to become and stay Christians: they feel loved by their parents. This insight has had a truly profound impact on my parenting. Love makes the biggest impact on our children's lives.

As moms, I believe we should all memorize the powerful verses of 1 Corinthians 13 because they not only describe love but also illustrate its actions:

> Though I speak with the tongues of men and of angels, but have not love, I have become sounding brass or a clanging cymbal. . . . And though I bestow all my goods to feed the poor, and though I give my body to be burned, but have not love, it profits me nothing.
>
> Love suffers long and is kind; love does not envy; love does not parade itself, is not puffed up;
>
> does not behave rudely, does not seek its own, is not provoked, thinks no evil;
>
> does not rejoice in iniquity, but rejoices in the truth;
>
> bears all things, believes all things, hopes all things, endures all things.
>
> Love never fails. . . .

When I was a child, I spoke as a child, I understood as a child, I thought as a child; but when I became a man, I put away childish things. For now we see in a mirror, dimly. . . . Now I know in part, but then I shall know just as I also am known.

And now abide faith, hope, love, these three; but the greatest of these is love. (NKJV)

My mother's last words to me in the hospital as she lay dying were, "I am so disappointed." Jesus does not want any mom to have this as her epitaph. What we do in love will endure. Jesus helped me to bear the burdens of life and taught me to not give up on loving my husband and my children. I can only see my own future dimly, but I can see God's love clearly. We belong to a Father who never gives up loving us.

Ponder

God's Word

This is love: not that we loved God, but that he loved us and sent his Son as an atoning sacrifice for our sins. (1 John 4:10)

Love comes from God. Everyone who loves is born of God and experiences a relationship with God. The person who refuses to love doesn't know the first thing about God, because God is love—so you can't know him if you don't love. This is how God showed his love for us: God sent his only Son into the world so we might live through him. This is the kind of love we are talking about—not that we once upon a time loved God, but that he loved us and sent his Son as a sacrifice to clear away our sins and the damage they've done to our relationship with God. (1 John 4:7–10 MSG)

Great are the works of the LORD; they are pondered by all who delight in them. . . . The fear of the LORD is the beginning of wisdom; all who follow his precepts have good understanding. To him belongs eternal praise. (Ps. 111:2, 10)

The Authors' Words

"The root in *belongs* is *longs*; every child longs to be at the center of his or her mom's and dad's hearts."

Assess

1. Are you confident of the Father's love for you?
2. How successful have you been in communicating a sense of love to your children's hearts? What can you do to improve in this area?
3. In what ways is God challenging you to love your children at the expense of yourself? Why is that difficult?
4. How deeply are you involved in your children's lives? Would any of your neighbors or friends describe you as uninvolved? Why or why not?
5. Would you say that love is the strongest or at least one of the strongest dynamics in your home? Would your husband? Would your children? Why or why not?

Sum Up

As Sigmund Freud argued, it is not attention that a child is seeking but love. Our children won't remember us as perfect; they will remember that we loved them.

Two

A United Family: Building Belonging

In Palo Alto, California, a neighborhood child a few years older than Sasha became a permanent fixture at our home for a period of several years. Her dad worked from home, and her mom was very busy pursuing a medical degree. Caroline would come to our home pretty much every day. At first Caroline was very demanding and whiny because she had experienced little parental supervision and care. Over time she understood the rules of our household and took on a softer demeanor. I also believe she felt our prayers for her and appreciated our sincere concern for her welfare. The fact that she could eat as much as she wanted probably also helped.

Caroline's dad died suddenly of a drug overdose at age forty-three, leaving the family in total disarray. On the night of his death, Caroline was having dinner at our house. The moment I answered the door and saw her mom's face I knew something dreadful had occurred. Caroline resisted her mom's insistent demands to come home. On our front door steps, her mom had to tell Caroline the shocking truth that her dad had died. Caroline gave me a longing look as she left with her mom. Caroline came back within the hour to sleep over, and we prayed with her and shared the truth of the Bible. In the hour of her greatest need Caroline felt she belonged with us, rather than with her mother.

We went to the New Age memorial service for Caroline's father. I will never forget the fabrications that were served up to justify his life and tragic death: "He was a free spirit." "He was a great dad who let his children find their own path." "He really loved his kids." Unfortunately, these platitudes were completely untrue.

A short time after this we moved to Virginia. It was very sad to leave Caroline behind. In the years that followed, Caroline started using drugs, just like her father. We heard from her less and less; it was clear that her life wasn't going in the right direction. She was left to fend for herself as her mom pursued her professional goals. A few years later my husband saw Caroline in the old neighborhood during a business trip to Silicon Valley. Her eyes were glassy and her speech was slurred. She had been a lively and bright young girl who just wanted to be loved and to belong. These she did not receive at home so she had found substitutes. Without some type of divine intervention, her life is very likely to follow the path of her father's.

We all need to feel loved and that we belong. Children who do not feel loved and who have no sense of belonging start life with a huge burden. The devastation created by parents who have effectively given up on their children is all around us. Many kids never recover.

At the end of this last school year, I attended a meeting at my son's middle school to discuss various issues. Toward the end of the meeting, I asked one of the educators about the coming eighth-grade year. She was open about the fact that eighth grade is a difficult year because of puberty and the fact that many kids are plain unhappy. This trend continues with often tragic results at our local high school. The educator believes this unhappiness is a direct result of parents leading separate lives to those of their kids. Modern parents in increasing numbers are more intent on doing their own thing as individuals rather than serving their families. Unfortunately, this leads to kids raising themselves, often with disastrous results.

How do we as parents give our children the strength they need to put love and wisdom into practice? The truth is that the sense of belonging that comes from a strong family will be a fountain of strength for each of our children for their entire lives. Our kids' future emotional fortitude depends heavily on their knowing they are unconditionally loved by their parents and they will never be rejected within the family. This sense of belonging will be a wellspring of hope for their future and a source of strength even when times grow tough, as they do for us all at certain points in our lives.

Moms need a fresh dose of strength, hope, and joy every day. Amid the dirty laundry, the constant cooking and cleaning, the unending bills, and the overflowing demands of our time, how do we find the hope and the joy we need to have strength for the journey? All of us want to know how to build a strong and united family in the face of cultural forces that are challenging families everywhere.

Building a strong and united family goes back to the fundamental question of belonging. First and foremost this is a question for ourselves. Do we understand that we are part of something much, much greater than the daily routine and that we are the Lord's creation? For me, it was essential to recognize that I have been entrusted by our heavenly Father with building His kingdom and His glory on this earth in the next generation. My main ministry to my family is to be the expression of the arms of the Lord to my husband and our children.

Moms are God's hands of love and His voice of joy to our families. Each one of us is fundamental to God's plan for this earth. In the same way that our children belong to us, we belong to our heavenly Father. Just as we have hopes and dreams for our children, our Father has hopes and dreams for us. His dreams are not the false siren call of material comfort or worldly fame. Even those who are enthralled by worldly riches and success must admit it will all pass away, which is why so many people keep seeking more and more as they grow dissatisfied with what they already have. Living the reality of belonging to our heavenly Father is fundamental to everything else. Just as our children know they can count on us, we know that we can count on our Father every day because we belong to Him.

My life would have been incomparably easier if we had placed our three-year-old in preschool the year we lived in Virginia. I would have been free from a child at the hip while I taxied the older kids to school, unpacked dozens of boxes, supervised an extensive renovation, and buddied up with our daughter Sasha. But our little Nicky had been rattled by the move from California and I needed to be his stability. Throughout our many moves for Gregory's career, my staying at home proved the wisest course of action for our family. I have worked from home, but ultimately the kids know that Mom can be found in the kitchen, in the garden, or at her desk. The older kids can count seven major family moves due to business relocation. At the same time, they have always known stability because they know exactly where their parents are and that we are in their corner. Obviously we've made our share of mistakes, but our children have a place of love and safety that is our family. This sense of security makes all the difference for children.

SEARCHING FOR A SENSE OF BELONGING

We all have dreams, and women are all born with a desire and need to satisfy our creativity. And we want the same for our children. This is a wonderful, healthy expression of our humanity. But ultimately it is not what we do that gives us meaning. A fellow venture capitalist in Silicon Valley once told my husband that his life was not very fulfilling. He loved his wife and would never be unfaithful; he adored his beautiful children and would never abandon them; and the success he had striven for was finally within his grasp—so why did he feel so empty? Because even with dreams fulfilled, creativity satisfied, we are created to belong to something even greater.

We have all been created to belong, to be closely related to others, for we are social creatures. This truth is echoed by the teachings of evolutionary biology and human psychology as well as by all major faiths, very much including Christianity. We all know that this is true. But the essential truth is only God can fill the empty space in our hearts. Some of us will smother this innate emptiness so we don't feel the ache. Some will try to fill the emptiness with the things of this world. But the reality is that parents and children want to know for today and for all eternity what their purpose is and to whom they belong. Purpose and the meaning of life are big questions we all must tackle if we are to be filled with peace and belonging.

Many people do not choose a life of faith. They may decide that the purpose of life is to belong to oneself. If this is true, then doing what feels best to make me happy should suffice. "It's all about me" is the guiding principle of this worldview. Unfortunately this modus operandi eventually leads to a feeling of emptiness and loneliness because we were fundamentally created to belong. I was like this. By belonging only to myself, I felt not only sad and lonely (ironic because I was popular and surrounded by people, especially men) but I was also worried that this sadness would pursue me my entire life. I suspected that by living for myself, I would be destined to die by myself. I also realized that I would end up hurting anyone who depended on my love, because I was much more intent on loving myself and satisfying myself. I had already witnessed, at close range, individuals who had chosen that path and it had played out like a tragedy. As the Bible teaches us, "Do not be deceived: God cannot be mocked. A man reaps what he sows" (Gal. 6:7).

I came to realize I desperately wanted to fill the longing in my heart to belong. This realization brought me to faith as I began to understand that I belonged to our heavenly Father. Through Jesus' death for me, I was brought into belonging to His family of believers and to my own family. In this, I have found great joy.

THE COVENANT OF MARRIAGE: THE STRENGTH OF BELONGING

The covenant of marriage is one of belonging. The power of the marriage covenant is the primary foundation for a happy family.

Marriage is not a contract: "If you do such and such I will do so and so . . . but if you do not I will not." And it is not pie-in-the-sky: "I will be madly in love with you for the rest of my life." The marriage covenant is many things, but most fundamentally it is a covenant of belonging. The Bible teaches us that "a man leaves his father and mother and is united [belongs] to his wife" (Gen. 2:24). In a mystical but very real way, marriage brings a man and a woman together in a covenant that is made to withstand the vicissitudes of life.

So if you are married, you belong to your husband in the same way he belongs to you. That means he cares for you as he cares for his own person. It means you care for him in that same way. This is a high and holy calling for husband and wife.

If your marriage (or mine) isn't measuring up right now, the right answer is not to lower the goal. The right answer is to find ways to get back to that state of intimacy and true belonging. This sense of belonging is the foundation upon which strong families are built. Furthermore, one of the most important gifts we can give our children is to show them what a good marriage looks like. Given the reality of human nature, building a good marriage through the years is not easy. However, the value that resides in marriage makes everything we put into it worthwhile. And if you're a single mom, do not give in to worry. You belong to the Lord and He to you. In fact, He's given you a special promise in the book of Isaiah: "[The Lord] gently leads those that have young" (40:11).

Our children belong to us, and they know this from the womb. Immediately at birth they turn for love and sustenance in our arms. And we belong to them. If we're fortunate enough to have a faithful husband, we need to thank God for him every day. He's not perfect for sure. But we need to give thanks for our husband and be sure he knows how much we appreciate him. He belongs to you via the vows that you both took before God and your closest friends and family. He also belongs to you because through your union, God has created new life. In very real spiritual ways you belong to your children and your husband, and they to you. This reality gives us joy and strength.

The fact that we belong to our family, and they to us, means something very important for us as moms. It means that we are not alone. It means there is a purpose and a meaning to life that is beyond just living for ourselves. And deep in our soul we know that is right. I came to motherhood with a belief that motherhood is valuable, that I wanted to be a mother, and that my ministry to my family would connect me to something and Someone much greater than myself.

MOTHERS AND A SENSE OF BELONGING IN THE MODERN WORLD

Women are supposedly freer today than their counterparts of one hundred years ago: free to be, free to choose, free to do whatever we want. This freedom is supposed to make us happier—but in reality, many of us are more confused or conflicted than our grandmothers ever were. The measurements we take on come as a direct result of not knowing where, or to whom, we belong. I will return to this issue of measurements many times in this book because I believe that all of us were created to have meaning and significance in our lives. But instead of taking on eternal aspirations and wise measurements for ourselves, we tend to take on those our culture tells us will validate us. As a result we are passing on the brokenness that results from misplaced aspirations and measurements to our children in a way that will haunt them.

Who are you as a woman? As a mom? What do you believe and where do you stand on the gritty issues of life? From the first step into marriage and motherhood, it is essential that moms feel the value of who they are. God values us, and our families need us. We all need to know deep in our souls that we are to be a tremendous blessing to our families, even if at times our families don't acknowledge that fact.

If we do not embrace motherhood as a spiritual ministry and a high calling from God, the world will beat us down. There have been many times I have felt invisible because I don't work outside the home. I didn't think others perceived what I did as valuable. But as the old saying goes: "What you see depends on where you stand." If we stand with our heavenly Father, we will learn to see things as He does. We will see the eternal importance of the role He has entrusted to us as a mom.

If we do not have a sense of greater purpose and a sense of belonging, we will struggle as moms in a society where a successful career and self-actualization are preeminent virtues. We will chafe against the sacrifices required by motherhood. It is a confusing twenty-first century for many mothers, especially young mothers. Our culture tells women we are entitled to our own happiness, including my career, my body, my latte, my workout, and so on. But when we have children, sacrifice becomes part of the package. Understanding that our lives have meaning in an eternal perspective gives moms the vision to stay the course, even when struggles come.

BELONGING AND THE GREAT CROWD OF WITNESSES

Prior generations faced the challenge of sheer survival, but they believed they belonged within a spiritual sphere. Men and women not only understood their position in society but they also understood they had a connection to the divine. They drew great comfort from their belief that their earthly existence was an integral part of God's great plan. Seeing this life as preparation for eternity changes the entire dynamic of our lives. Being raised in a secular generation spiritually impoverishes all of us, including our children. I think many of us mistakenly look back at earlier generations with pity.

Modern conveniences and wealth don't make it easier for us to worship God; in fact these can serve as distractions. The great French mathematician Pascal observed that in every human heart there is an emptiness that only God can fill with His Son, Jesus Christ. Only when our empty hearts are filled with God will we find significance and meaning. Our ministry as moms will lead the way for our kids to experience the same fulfillment.

In Hebrews 11 and 12, Paul passionately urged Christians who were being brutally persecuted to remember that we as believers all belong to a "great cloud of witnesses" (12:1). These brothers and sisters were not just being thrown in jail, but they were being tortured and killed for their faith. They needed spiritual strength in the face of such sacrifice. Remembering that Christians belong to God, and to each other, strengthens us. Moms have to draw on these reminders, as we often feel embattled in times of difficulty and stress. We belong to a long line of faithful brethren stretching back to Abraham and beyond. This "great cloud of witnesses" has grown immeasurably in the past two thousand years, cheering us on. We belong to this heavenly family, and now is our time to have an impact for the kingdom of God on this generation.

God does not reject us, His children. We cannot let rejection be the future of our children. It is essential that we give them the security that only a stable family can bring, no matter our individual circumstance. Single moms are pushed in ways unimaginable to married moms, but stability has to be a prime focus.

My father always said that children are the most conservative creatures in the world; there is much wisdom to this. Kids like what they know and who they know since it brings them security and a sense of comfort. Our kids do not get their peace and security from worldly markers of success. Knowing that they belong, no matter what, is what our kids value and require. Belonging gives our children the strength they need to weather the storms of life. Just as importantly, it will give them the sense that their lives have significance and meaning. They are created for something only they were uniquely created to do here on earth.

Ponder

God's Word

> Two are better than one,
> because they have a good return for their labor:
> If either of them falls down,
> one can help the other up. (Eccles. 4:9–10)

You are a chosen people, a royal priesthood, a holy nation, God's special possession, that you may declare the praises of him who called you out of darkness into his wonderful light. (1 Pet. 2:9)

> From everlasting to everlasting
> the LORD's love is with those who fear him,
> and his righteousness with their children's children—
> with those who keep his covenant
> and remember to obey his precepts. (Ps. 103:17–18)

The Authors' Words

"If we do not embrace motherhood as a spiritual ministry and a high calling from God, the world will beat us down."

Assess

1. How strong is your sense of belonging to God's family? Why is that? What might you do to strengthen your understanding of that reality?
2. Do you see yourself as God's minister to your family? Do you believe this is an important role in God's kingdom? Why or why not?
3. In what practical ways can you build a sense of belonging in your family? Spiritual disciplines? Holiday traditions? Family fun?
4. Do you feel that your marriage is more like a covenantal relationship (I will love you no matter what) or a contractual relationship (I will do X and Y if you do A and B)? Why? How does your spouse feel? Why? Would you like to change that? If so, how?
5. How does the knowledge that you belong to God's family affect your attitudes and behavior as a mother?

Sum Up

Family belonging is critical to the development of our children's identity and security. The greater world can be a chaotic and incomprehensible place for our kids, but the stability we provide when they walk through the front door will act as a buffer and foundation that won't disappoint.

Three

The Importance of Vision: Thriving Families

A re you and your husband committed to a common vision for your family? I don't mean the small details of where you will go on vacation or what kind of car you will drive. The phrase "the devil is in the details" is insightful, because the devil is the one who wants us to focus on the details: the small ruptures, the differences in approach, and the daily grind. Even when the big vision is clear, the frustrating details of life may fog the overall picture. Your family vision calls you to something bigger than yourselves. The devil wants us to focus on the small, petty details of life because he wants us to be small people who raise kids to live small, stagnant lives.

Proverbs 29:18 tells us, "Where there is no vision, the people perish" (KJV). Likewise, a family who does not share a vision for its future is at risk of eventually perishing. My husband and

I are committed to each other, to our children, and to our faith. We share a common vision for our family's future. This vision helps us weather the storms all families go through. It helps us to prioritize our commitment to each other and to our kids, and it encourages us not to be overly discouraged when mistakes are made. Gregory and I have chosen to embrace not only the successes, but also the failures of life. Through our shared vision we have placed ourselves in agreement, because as the Old Testament teaches us, "Can two walk together, unless they are agreed?" (Amos 3:3 NKJV). And as Jesus Himself told us, "If a house is divided against itself, that house cannot stand" (Mark 3:25).

At this point in your family life, do you have the same overarching vision for your family's future as your husband does? Have you ever talked about this essential question? How about your children, especially if they are over the age of twelve? They are developing a vision for their own futures, with or without your help. Do they know what your family vision is? Do you know what their personal vision is? A common vision is a powerful unifying force for a family. It can help us get through tough times together. A family vision reminds family members what is truly important, and what is not. It acts as a unifier and a safety net.

How can we, as mothers, establish a family vision that each member of our family shares? Certainly it is critical to get your husband onboard. He is called to be the servant leader for your family, but you may need to be the initiator. The truth is that establishing a common vision for your family's future may start with you.

So what is your family vision? In other words, what do you

want your family to look like in ten years, twenty years, thirty years? And what are you, as coleader of your family, doing to make sure you get there together?

Perhaps you haven't really thought about a vision for your family's future. Or maybe you have a bit of a vision, but you've not shared it with your husband and kids. That is common—in fact, few families have a shared family vision. Most families have a financial plan, and many families think ahead about their children's education. That makes sense, because in this world nothing truly meaningful is ever done by accident. No great literature or work of art was ever created by accident. "Time and chance," for good and ill, play a part in all of human life (Eccles. 9:11). But there is no significant human accomplishment of any kind that did not start with a vision and a plan.

A family vision is a plan of action based on shared beliefs and hopes of where you want to go as a family. It solidifies your family philosophy and articulates the goals and aspirations you all share. I will share with you our Slayton Noble Family Vision at the end of this chapter. But this is ours—every family must develop its own. Half the benefit is in working on it together, and the other half is seeing it come to pass by God's grace.

A SHARED VISION FOR YOUR FAMILY'S FUTURE

Vision, in good times and bad, keeps families moving forward together. It helps us keep our eyes on the ultimate goal. In that same way, a shared vision can help families succeed. A shared vision gives every member of the family a stronger sense of belonging to something greater than himself or herself. This helps especially in stressful periods. A shared family vision helps us not to give in and not to give up on ourselves or each other.

Building a vision for your family's future isn't something you do in a day. But it is something you can start today. Over time, you can build a vision of what you want your family to be down the road of time. Then you can share it with your husband and children and get their input. Remember, getting everyone's input—and making it a shared family vision—is absolutely key.

The interesting thing about a family vision is that even though it can be extremely helpful for a family's long-term happiness and fulfillment, it is not something most couples spend any time thinking about. When tough times come—as they do for every family—a shared vision can be the difference between saving your family or seeing it ripped apart. This is why it is so important for you to establish a clear, shared family vision. There are many competing priorities today. A shared family vision serves to keep a family focused on what is important in life, and what is not. In twenty or thirty years, that can be the difference between a happy family and a bunch of shattered dreams.

WITHOUT A VISION THE FAMILY PERISHES

At the extreme end of shattered families are suicides. Teenage suicides are at record levels, with suicides the third leading cause of death among fifteen- to twenty-four-year-olds, and the fourth leading cause of death between the ages of ten and fourteen.[1] Why do kids take their lives? There are many factors, of course, some of which are beyond a family's control. What is in our control is the sense of value and belonging we give to our children by pointing to their integral role in our family and community, and also in God's. It is critical that they know they have been created to play an important role in this world even as they come to grips with the fact that neither they, nor we, are at its center.

One of our son's high school classmates committed suicide. Bob came home every day after school and had little to do. His parents were divorced and both were busy with full-time jobs and new partners. Bob was a stutterer, and he was mocked at school for his speech impediment. The family was shocked by the suicide, but Bob's peers knew what was going on. Bob felt totally alone in his suffering. Our son had faced bullying at a private school in Bermuda, so he has developed both a sixth sense and a compassion for others in the same situation. Even though there was little overlap in their schedules, our son made sure to include Bob when he could. Bob was a really lonely child. He did not have a sport or musical activity after school. He had been a latchkey kid for years. Bob was isolated during the afterschool hours that are so critical to teenagers.

Bob was feeling confused and out of place in a strange home with a new stepdad, new stepsiblings, and a busy mom who was not home much. The adults around Bob wanted to focus on the fact that he was "functioning." He was going to school regularly, he could be counted on to be at home after school, and he wasn't getting into serious trouble. The parents chose to believe everything was fine. They may not have known about the bullying; sometimes teenagers don't want to share painful episodes with their parents. Had they been paying closer attention, they would have known that their son was in trouble and needed their help. Bob had no vision for his life either within the family or beyond it. Teenagers need to have a vision—a sense of where they come from, where they are going, and what they can accomplish. A life vision is a large part of the legacy children receive from their parents. Bob's suicide is a tragedy. It was the result of a life without belonging and without vision.

A family vision helps parents create a worldview that gives their kids a sense of place and purpose. We want our kids to know that they are integral parts of the family, with a role only they can fulfill in the family. Communicating with children to discuss a family's purpose and plan helps give our kids a sense that they have a role in life, that life is valuable, and that they are part of something greater than themselves. As they grow older, they will have more input into shaping the family vision. Eventually they will develop their own family vision, a process made much easier if they have experienced living in a family that has one.

BUILDING YOUR SHARED FAMILY VISION

You and your spouse should take a few minutes to begin developing a shared family vision. It's not hard; in fact, it is a lot of fun. It will help you remember why you wanted to be a family in the first place and what you have to look forward to. No matter where you are as a family, a shared family vision can help. If you and your husband are expecting your first child, this is a perfect time to make sure you share a vision for your family's future. If your kids are almost off to college or work—even if they are already out of the nest—a shared family vision can help you develop a common idea of what you want your larger family, including grandchildren, to look like in the future.

Here are five questions to help you build your shared family vision. Answer these questions in the context of where you want to be in ten, twenty, and thirty years:

1. What kind of relationship do you want to have with your husband ten, twenty, and thirty years from now? How do you want to interact and relate with him? What do you want your marriage to look like? What do you hope he will say about you as a wife and a mother?

2. What kind of parents do you and your husband want to be? What do you want your children, when they are grown, to remember about your family life together? How would you like them to characterize their childhood?

3. What do you want your kids to be like when they are adults? How do you want your children to relate to their own spouses and children? What kind of husband or wife—and mom or dad—do you want your children to be?

4. How do you want your children to interact with each other in the future—and with each other's families? How do you want your children to interact with you and your husband in the future? What kind of relationship do you hope to have with your grown children?

5. What are the core values that help bind your family together? What do you all believe is truly important in life? How will you nurture your common faith—and how might that faith help your family stick together?

When you've answered these questions you will have the basic outline of your family vision. While you don't have to answer each of these questions right now, we encourage you to grab a pen or your laptop and write down as many answers as you can. It won't take you long, and as you write you will begin an important process that could have a great impact on your future.

When you've written down your answers, please take time to meditate on them, refine them, and share them with your husband first, and when you are both ready, with your kids. You may even want to discuss them with a close friend or your spiritual adviser. Over time, add connecting phrases to make your answers into a unified statement, instead of five different answers. Little by little, you will be creating your own family vision.

Don't worry that it's not perfect. Write down a first draft, no matter how rough it might be, and you'll be halfway there. There is a reason all great stories get recorded: the written word lasts. God gave the Ten Commandments to Moses in written form because the written word has staying power, and it has guiding power. Writing a family vision will be a very important conversation you have with your spouse, with the Lord, and with your family.

Get Your Family Onboard

You should create a vision for your entire family, not just for you. So here's a suggestion. Invite your husband out for a special dinner and get his thoughts, ideas, and (eventually) his buy-in. A family vision can't work without your husband's full partnership, so get his input from the start. By the way, if you don't have a husband, a family vision that you share with your children can also be a very powerful tool. So don't put it off if you are single. It is still vital for your family.

Once you have a shared family vision written down, it's time for a family meeting. For your children, lay out the vision for them in a way they can understand. It must be age-appropriate to be effective. Discuss it with them, and see if they have any suggestions or changes. Each child has an important role in making your family vision a reality. If the kids have good ideas about how to make the vision even stronger, be sure to incorporate them. The results of the meeting might be surprising. If you have teenagers, it probably won't be the easiest discussion; to be honest, that was the case for us. Regardless, laying out your family vision for your kids and asking for their help will ensure that they are part of the endeavor. If sharing and discussing the family vision is done with kindness and humor, it will draw you together as a family.

Once you've all agreed on your family vision, finalize it in writing and have everyone sign it. If possible, have it written up nicely and framed. Put it where the whole family will see it frequently. At least twice a year, call a family meeting to ask, "How are we doing on our family vision?" Keep the vision in your family's minds; don't let it fade into the background. With the passage of time, your family vision may require modification. But the fact that you have explicitly made it a family priority will have practical benefits down the road. It will help each member of your family better understand where you are going as a team—and where you want to end up.

A family vision is especially valuable in the tough times. A family vision can serve as glue when the way going forward seems unclear and not very rewarding. Of course without effective leadership even the noblest vision isn't much better than a dream. But with true servant leadership and a shared family vision, your family can persevere and experience a beautiful future.

Our family vision has helped us in many important areas.

One of the most critical has been in helping to break bad choices that existed in both our families. As we will talk about in the next chapter, most of us tend to struggle in the same areas our parents did. In my husband's family alcoholism, adultery, and bankruptcy have haunted the last four generations. For us it has been essential to become the generational firewall that will allow our children to break free of these patterns and go further in the Lord's wisdom and maturity than we have. Having a shared family vision has helped us to do just that.

As I promised to do, I want to share with you our Noble Family Vision. Again, please do not think of this as some kind of perfect model; it is not. But hopefully it will help you and your family come up with your own. And may our heavenly Father help you and your family see your shared family vision come to pass!

The Slayton Noble Family Vision

We are—and will strive to be—a family that serves the Lord, each other, and our community for good. As we all grow up together we will do everything we can to preserve and to deepen the bonds between us, bonds of faith and blood and love and joy. We will treat each other with kindness, always believing the best about each other. We will give each other the benefit of the doubt and will stick up for each other in thick or thin, no matter what.

As parents, we will put our children's and grandchildren's character, soul, and future ahead of our own needs and desires.

We will work hard for them and pray for them continually. May God help us be the very best parents we can be.

As the younger generation, we commit to living lives of integrity, courage, and honor. We know that to do that will require God's help—so we will continue to seek His blessing and His guidance in all we do. We will seek to marry noble spouses who are strong in faith, rich in love, and deep in wisdom. We will raise our own children in the love and wisdom of the Lord, as our Mom and Dad have tried their best to do for us. And we will do everything we can to strengthen and deepen the bonds of family down through the generations, no matter how many miles or time zones we might have to cross.

Once married, we will not divorce. We will honor the example our own parents set for us by talking out our differences, praying diligently for one another, and serving one another as Christ Himself served us. We will have a Noble Family Vision of our own—which will be in some ways different from this one. But in the most important elements we will do our best to pass on to our children that which our parents passed on to us: the love and faith and joy and peace that come from a happy family and the blessings of God Almighty.

In the years to come, we will continue to honor our parents by caring for them as they cared for us when we were young. They did not outsource us to nannies or boarding schools. We will not outsource them to old age homes or institutions . . . no matter what.

Holy God of heaven, help us to see this vision come to pass, no matter what happens. Give us the courage, the wisdom, and the love to build a strong and happy family. And many years from now, may we all look back from heaven at our life together with joy and the quiet satisfaction of a race well run.

Ponder

God's Word

> Where there is no revelation [vision], people cast off
> restraint;
> but blessed is the one who heeds wisdom's instruction.
> (Prov. 29:18)
> We will tell the next generation
> the praiseworthy deeds of the LORD,
> his power, and the wonders he has done.
> He decreed statutes for Jacob
> and established the law in Israel,
> which he commanded our ancestors
> to teach their children,
> so the next generation would know them,
> even the children yet to be born,
> and they in turn would tell their children.
> Then they would put their trust in God
> and would not forget his deeds
> but would keep his commands. (Ps. 78:4–7)

> Can two walk together, unless they are agreed? (Amos
> 3:3 NKJV)

The Authors' Words

"There is no significant human accomplishment of any
kind that did not start with a vision and a plan. A family vision

is a plan of action based on shared beliefs and hopes of where you want to go as a family. It solidifies your family philosophy and articulates the goals and aspirations you all share."

Assess

1. On the continuum between a solid, healthy family and a completely shattered family, where is yours? And which direction are you headed in? Why?
2. Do you believe God can help you and your family move in the right direction? Why or why not?
3. Do you see yourself as a leader—a vision communicator—to your family? Have you communicated your family vision with them?
4. Do you and your spouse and children have a shared family vision? Do you talk about it from time to time? Is it real in your life as a family? Why or why not?
5. If you don't have a shared family vision, will you use the five questions on page 35 to craft a shared family vision? If not, why not?

Sum Up

Even politicians like Bill Clinton quote the verse "Where there is no vision, the people perish" because we cannot go forward if we don't have a goal and a strategy to get there. Establishing vision for the entire family will bolster our children's sense of belonging and identity. At the same time, a family vision points the way forward, especially during difficult seasons of life.

Four

Breaking Generational Curses: Wholeness Is Possible

Kara began life with a difficult history. Her parents were divorced, and there was no financial help from her dad; in fact, the last time she saw her dad was when she was nine. Her mother was an alcoholic more interested in men than in her. Growing up, Kara felt that she had no stability. Kara moved out of state when she was eighteen. She worked as hard as she could to build success, and just as hard to deny her past. She lied to friends, coworkers, and even to her daughter about her past. Her first and second marriages ended in divorce, and she saw in her daughter history repeating itself.

Kara helplessly watched her daughter doing badly in school, running after boys, and most hurtful of all, turning away from her mom. Kara herself was turning more and more to alcohol. Kara knew that she and her daughter could not go on like this.

Kara's work was a restful place for her because she did not have to talk about anything personal. She felt her time at the office was an oasis. She was irked because a coworker who had recently become a Christian insisted on sharing the gospel with her. At lunch, Kara regularly chose to sit elsewhere when she saw Mary. One day, however, Kara could no longer deny her feelings of despair. She saw Mary at the business cafeteria and deliberately sat beside her. She simply asked about Mary's church. That Sunday, Kara and her very reluctant daughter went to church. Thus began a several-year odyssey to bring reconciliation and redemption to their lives. Kara stopped masking her hurt with alcohol, and she received counseling. Her daughter found in the youth group the meaning and acceptance she had been seeking. One of the most important areas of healing Kara experienced was to be released from the shame she grew up with. Shame that her father was not around; shame that her mother was a drunk; shame that she could not present a happy picture of her childhood. She became free of the generational curses that had been sinking her life.

Kara's deepest healing came in the area of rejection. Because she had been rejected by her parents, she rejected them and her husbands. But God does not reject the broken; in fact, it became clear to Kara that acceptance is one of the central ministries of Jesus. As Christ Himself said,

The Spirit of the LORD is upon Me,
Because He has anointed Me
To preach the gospel to the poor;
He has sent Me to heal the brokenhearted,
To proclaim liberty to the captives

And recovery of sight to the blind,
To set at liberty those who are oppressed. (Luke 4:18 NKJV).

This is the fulfillment of Isaiah 61:1. Jesus had come to heal Kara and to set her free from the generational curses that had dogged the women in her family for generations. God does not abandon the brokenhearted; on the contrary, through His healing love He gives us the power to move forward without a sense of shame and defeat.

BREAKING GENERATIONAL CURSES

We are called to protect our children by breaking, with God's help, the cycles of brokenness we often inherit from past generations. Whether we call it genetic predisposition or intergenerational transfer, many of us tend to suffer from and repeat the worst tendencies of our forefathers. Gregory and I had to look carefully at the issue of generational patterns from a spiritual angle to avoid repeating the same destructive problems in our own family. Generational curses are ultimately broken by Jesus, for as it is written in the great prophetic chapter of Isaiah 53,

> Surely He has borne our griefs
> And carried our sorrows. . . .
> He was wounded for our transgressions,
> He was bruised for our iniquities . . .
> And by His stripes we are healed." (vv. 4–5 NKJV)

Ultimately it is through Christ's power that we experience healing from generational curses, but we must walk in obedience to unlearn tendencies picked up from our parents. Through prayer and discernment we allow the Holy Spirit to minister to our deepest hurts. By not having dialogue with temptation and walking according to holiness we open the door to God's redemptive power in our lives.

Many in our parents' and grandparents' generations assumed that the culture and tradition of their families and society would give them the ability to raise a functioning family. That may have been true in pro-family cultures of the past; but for most families today this simply doesn't work. Today the strong Judeo-Christian cultural traditions and social morals that helped our grandparents raise their families are mostly gone. Our society no longer emphasizes the morality or ethics our children need to make sound decisions.

As a result, generational curses may be more prevalent today than in earlier generations. But with the Lord's direction and help, these destructive generational tendencies can be changed for good. A conscious decision through prayer and discernment on the part of the parents to do things differently is the key first step to healing past behavioral patterns. My husband and I determined that there were certain disciplines we would have to incorporate into our lives in order to become a generational firewall for our children. While we certainly have not done any of these perfectly, these actions have greatly helped us and our children in ways big and small.

There are necessary steps to begin the path to His grace. Let us begin with the first step. We must repent of our sins and ask the Lord Jesus to cleanse us by His blood. Recognition of sin is imperative: both that sin exists and that we are sinners. I recognized that it is only by the atonement of Jesus that I could be saved. Over time I have tried to bring all my heavy burdens to the Cross because I knew that it would only be at His feet that I could receive Jesus' beautiful promise: "Come to me, all you who are weary and burdened, and I will give you rest" (Matt. 11:28).

Over the years, Jesus has freed me of the burdens of unforgiveness, anger, and bitterness. He can do the same for you and your family. I also have to admit that because Jesus is gracious, He does not reveal all at once the various burdens we carry. It is only with the passage of time that the layers unfold and we can release them to God. Humility, honesty, and openness to the Lord are essential to healing.

It is essential that we recognize our failings and repent of them. We cannot spend our lives blaming others, even those from whom we have inherited these tendencies. We must take ownership of our issues. As we move forward we must do our best to walk daily in obedience to the Scriptures and to grow in the fruit of the Spirit: "love, joy, peace, forbearance, kindness, goodness, faithfulness, gentleness and self-control" (Gal. 5:22–23). These are powerful gifts indeed. The Holy Spirit is the secret weapon we must employ if we are to have victory against generations of complex, deep-seated issues. The Holy Spirit will help us when we humbly ask for His help and sincerely obey His Word and His leadings.

Godly, professional counseling can be extremely helpful. I have been deeply blessed through counseling. My counselor and I worked together on recognizing the generational curses that I had long wrestled with. She helped me to better understand them and give them over to God. Over time this helped me experience true release, which has been a real blessing for me and our family. However, there are many charlatans out there posing as counselors of one type or another. So be careful. This is where it's crucial to be in strong communities of wise women who can give sound advice.

THE GENERATIONAL CURSE OF FAVORITISM

Favoritism is as old as time. In the Bible, study the lives of Abraham and Sarah, Ishmael and Isaac, Isaac and Rebekah, Jacob and the sons of his wives and concubines. Each generation in turn chose a different son to favor and spoil. As a direct result of this rejection, envy and bitterness poisoned multiple generations. In a recently published book called *The Sibling Effect*, the author asserts that 70 percent of fathers and 65 percent of all moms evidence favoritism.[1]

The power of the Holy Spirit released Gregory and me from the curse of favoritism, which has been pervasive and destructive on both sides of the family. If my husband and I were to be asked what is the greatest strength of our family, we would both state without hesitation that it is the love our children bear for one another. God's power of healing and forgiveness allowed us to transform old family patterns, and His love paved the way for our family to develop healthier ways of interacting.

Our four children have the attitude of the Three Musketeers: all for one, and one for all. There is no tension when they are together. They do not compete with each other, nor are they jealous of each other's successes. Our kids love spending time with each other, and they like nothing better than family vacations. Given our extended families' issues with sibling rivalry caused by parental favoritism, this is a miracle that we don't take for granted. We know that it is the work of the Holy Spirit in the lives of our children, and it is beautiful.

A parent who chooses to honor one child over the others sets in motion a train wreck. The child who is disfavored will either come to dislike the parents or to fear his or her parents' judgment. The favored child also does not benefit. Jealousy is corrosive, and a jealous sibling is a dangerous person to have in one's life.

By giving in to a curse like favoritism, we are also depriving our children of one of the most important relationships of their lives: the sustaining friendship of their siblings. There is no one like your brother or sister with whom to share memories, laugh about old stories, and smile over past experiences. These qualities make brothers and sisters potentially the best friends anyone could ever have. Sadly, this was not the reality for my extended family, but it is for our nuclear family. We worked diligently as parents to let our children know that we love each of them equally.

Favoritism may not be a generational pattern in your extended family, but everyone, even from the healthiest families, has patterns that may not seem so bad in one generation, but if we'll allow them to take root they can become a cancer in the next generation or the generation after that. It is imperative to be honest about generational patterns in your family lines or bad habits you and your spouse have acquitted recently. If you deal with them openly, with God's help you can be healed. Otherwise, you or your children could be doomed to be mastered by them.

Healing from Generational Curses with God's Love

If you need love and power to break the generational curses that have come down from your forefathers, look to God. He has all the love and all the power you need for yourself and your family. But to fully access that love and power, He asks us to forgive those who hurt us. Yes, we need to forgive our parents—and all those who have failed us—wherever needed. The discipline of forgiveness is an essential key to the healing process. In my own case, my anger was not simply directed at my mother but at the Lord. I had prayed over and over for God to heal my relationship with my mom. I had generously opened my home to my mom, and we as a family had shown her love and respect. Even at her death, my mother left a deeply wounding letter criticizing Gregory, of all people. Gregory, who had always prayed for her and was so generous to her financially and spiritually.

So what did I do with all this bitterness? I don't have any easy answers, except that day by day I came to God and asked for the desire to forgive. It is the power of the Holy Spirit that allows us to forgive and be redeemed. He frees us from the burden of repeating the mistakes of prior generations. Of course, I have my issues. I have had to deal with bad habits that are hard to break. My mom was a screamer, and not surprisingly, I shout when upset. But I am able to smile at the future because I know God is using time as my friend and He is healing me of the past.

In my own healing process, I have had to give up blaming my mom and instead to learn to forgive her from my heart. This has been hugely freeing for me, as if I finally can live my own life no longer haunted by her specter. I have come to believe that not blaming is as powerful as forgiving. I no longer blame my mom or feel that I have to reject all that has come before. There is much good that came from my parents' legacy, good that I want to pass on to my own children as their inheritance. I could not recognize this truth until I took off the blinders of unforgiveness and bitterness.

I can now bless my mom, which has been a tremendous release for me. I can see the many strengths she had. She was a terrific cook and homemaker who really came alive when we had guests in our home. The root word for *guest* in Slavic languages shares the same root as the Slavic word for *God*. So guests in my parents' cultures were seen as from God. I have really benefited from her example in opening our home to so many guests and visitors, and it has been a blessing to my husband and our children that I can do so. So many of their friends have no welcoming home to come to. I am very appreciative of the fact that I am not intimidated by entertaining. My mother was also a source of wisdom, and I thank her for it.

I can easily bless my father because he understood forgiveness and did not give in to anger and bitterness. He loved our family and me very much. However, it was my father's example of being a good man who was powerless in the face of my mother's rage that helped me understand that only through God's power can we be transformed. My father loved my mother, but he could not save her from her demons. Without God's power, we are helpless in the face of the personal demons that haunt us.

Everyone goes through suffering. We cannot take offense at God for the sufferings we go through in this life. But we do. The Lord calls us to forgive those who have hurt us, especially those who have had a responsibility for us. Jesus underscores for us how important forgiveness is when He said on the cross: "Father, forgive them, for they do not know what they are doing" (Luke 23:34). That is the ultimate act of forgiveness and understanding. He wants us to do the same.

For some of us, our parents didn't know what they were doing. They trusted in culture or family tradition or Dr. Spock. Sometimes it worked, and sometimes it didn't. They did not set out to pass onto us their failures and fears, but in many cases they did. We must forgive them if we want to have any chance of breaking those generational curses and seeing our own children walk in freedom. It is no accident that the Lord instructed us to pray:

> Forgive us our debts,
> as we also have forgiven our debtors. (Matt. 6:12)

Since my mother is dead, I will never have the experience of having her ask for my forgiveness. I had to get over that fact. She will never acknowledge the deep pain she caused. The process of healing is often complicated by the fact that we want the people who have hurt us to ask for our forgiveness. We want them to recognize the great pain they caused us. These desires must be released to God. We must forgive and no longer cast blame because obedience is essential to healing. I thank God that I have come to a place of peace. Only the power of forgiveness unleashed by the Holy Spirit in my heart and mind has allowed me to do so.

DISAPPOINTMENT WITH THE LORD

Jesus said to John the Baptist in Luke 7:23: "Blessed is he who is not offended because of Me" (NKJV). It is very important to recognize if we are harboring any unforgiveness toward God. Most of us try to stuff these feelings down because we know that we should not be angry at God. But theory does not always translate into practice. In my honest moments, I saw that I was even angrier at God than I was at my mother. It has taken years of the Holy Spirit ministering to me for me to bless God for my childhood. I am truly at peace with what has happened. Recognizing how I felt about the Lord (and repenting!) has been instrumental in my healing process.

Many of us won't admit that we feel disappointed with God in some areas of our lives. I had to get on my knees for years to ask Him to put forgiveness in my heart for my mother. I also had to ask Him to help me not to be offended by the burdens He allowed me to bear as a child. God had to help me understand that while He created this world, He did not create its sin and brokenness. Despite everything in me and in this world that argues against it, I can trust Him. I can trust Him for healing, and I can trust Him to create in me wholeness.

I came to understand that time is my friend, not my enemy, in the healing process. What I had to do was give over the struggle to Jesus. I could not control the process of inner healing any more than I have been able to control the process of my physical healing. Currently, I can see from the example of my inner healing that I can trust the Lord for my physical healing. He knows what I need, and He has not forgotten that I am asking for health and wholeness. It has ironically been the journey of my inner healing that gives me the ability to see that God can do all things, but only if I allow the Holy Spirit to minister to me patience and faith. I understand that age and ill health are unavoidable, and I do not want to cringe at the thought of what is to come. But right now we have a youngster to get through middle and high school, and I am asking for complete physical healing. Thankfully I have already seen much answer to those prayers.

No matter what anyone says, there is no shortcut to inner healing. By God's grace, we bear witness to the fact that our God does heal. However, we must have faith in His goodness and in His promise that in all things He works for good for those who are called according to His purpose (Rom 8:28). When we walk in this healing faith, we begin to more fully unleash His healing power in our inner lives. But it takes time—His time.

GODLY OBEDIENCE: A KEY TO GROWTH

Godly obedience is an important topic in the Scriptures. Martin Luther loved to recite the simple verse that speaks of godly obedience: "The just shall live by faith" (Rom. 1:17 NKJV). If we truly want to live in the fullest sense of that verse, we must learn to walk in obedience to God's Spirit. The idea of obedience goes against some of the biggest idols in our culture (my independence, my rights, my freedom, my way, in short me, me . . . and oh yes, me). I cannot emphasize enough the blessings of walking with the Holy Spirit in obedience. There is no other way to walk with God closely.

I like to know where I am going and what I am doing. When I am lost, which happens more than I would like to admit, I usually use my determination to work harder to get unlost. Unfortunately this strategy doesn't work with our heavenly Father. When a sheep is lost, she needs the Shepherd to come and find her. The best strategy for the sheep is to stay close to the Shepherd. We must remember that we are like sheep in this regard. Being close to the Shepherd means we are where His strong and loving arms are closest, but it also means we are walking in obedience to Him. There is no other way. Jesus promised to send the Spirit to be our Helper and our Counselor and our Friend. We need all that help if we are going to have any hope of breaking the curses that have flowed down to us through the generations.

When we walk closely with His Spirit in obedience, He promises we will grow in the fruit of the Spirit: "love, joy, peace, forbearance, kindness, goodness, faithfulness, gentleness and self-control" (Gal. 5:22–23). During the hectic years of mothering, we will need all of these fruits. Perhaps one reason it is called fruit is because it is not only what we bear as we grow in godly character, but it also serves to nourish our family. Spiritual fruit is what our family feeds off of as we walk with God. Our spouses and children will feed from our patience and gentleness and self-control. I have mentioned that I have a tendency to scream when upset, and I can bear witness that no one feeds off my shouting. But I realized long ago that I cannot change the fundamentals about myself; only the Holy Spirit can. Thankfully, He is doing so.

GOD'S REFINING FIRES OF PAIN AND SUFFERING

Why does the Lord allow pain and suffering in this world He created? History's greatest minds have wrestled with that question, so I won't pretend to have a concise answer. But there is no doubt that our Father allows pain and suffering in part because it is in the most difficult times that we often learn the most about ourselves. In the very same way, it is in coming through the really tough times that we grow the most.

> The crucible for silver and the furnace for gold,
> but the LORD tests the heart.

This great verse, Proverbs 17:3, reminds us that our heavenly Father uses adversity and pain to refine our souls. Although it is not pleasant at the time, if we allow ourselves to be refined, the end result is good. In the end, God is removing the impurities from our own nature in order for us to be "blameless and pure" (Phil. 2:15).

It has taken very painful lessons to burn the dross from my soul. I still have much to learn, but I have grown in ways I never thought possible. Most importantly, I hope that my children will never have to worry about ending up broken and beaten like many of their forefathers. Our prayer is that they will walk in the freedom and maturity that Christ desires for all His people. Yes, it took some very difficult refining trials and there is still much work to do in my heart. But we serve a God who will never let us go unless we let Him go. He does not want us to remain spiritual babies, but to grow into the fullness and beauty of Christ, and to help lead our families there as well.

Early in our marriage, Gregory and I purposed that our primary ministry in raising our children would be to see them walk maturely in Christ, free from past generational curses. From the very beginning of our married life we both were aware of possible generational curses we would need to fight as a family. I needed to be honest with Gregory about them—after all, he would find out soon enough. He had a few of his own to share with me.

In an age-appropriate way we wanted to share these with our kids as well. We prayed together with our children for God's grace, discipline, and mercy. We not only prayed for our own family but for our extended family. We tried to keep our eyes on our long-term goals. Generational curses aren't broken in months or years but in decades and over lifetimes. So we have to keep the main goal in mind: to see the curse end in our generation and allow our children to walk in freedom and maturity.

The great news is that this is exactly our heavenly Father's intent. He moves with us and does not want us to suffer for the misdeeds of the prior generations. A family's problems can be opportunities for grace and mercy to flourish, since we were created by God to be overcomers and to raise overcomers. I can rejoice that my husband and I have found this to be true in our lives.

The Holy Spirit's power truly is the source of freedom from generational curses and sin. The fact that Gregory and I can point to twenty-six-plus years of a marriage that is growing and maturing is a miracle, given how many divorces are represented in both family lines. We are both strong-willed and come from broken families, but our God knows what He is doing. By bringing us through these years, He has shown again and again that He is able to redeem even the most difficult family situations. If He can do it for our family, He can surely transform yours.

Ponder

God's Word

Though my father and mother forsake me,
the LORD will receive me. (Ps. 27:10)
I have refined you, though not as silver;
I have tested you in the furnace of affliction. (Isa. 48:10)

He who began a good work in you will carry it on to
completion until the day of Christ Jesus. (Phil. 1:6)

The Authors' Words

"My husband and I determined that there were certain disciplines we would have to incorporate into our lives
in order to become a generational firewall for our children.
While we certainly have not done any of these perfectly,
these actions have greatly helped us and our children in
ways big and small."

Assess

1. Have you humbly recognized your failings and asked
   God's Holy Spirit to lead you into knowing and living
   in the Father's love?
2. Have you forgiven those who have failed you?
3. Have you and your spouse prayerfully and honestly
   talked about generational curses that might exist in

your family lines and what you can do to counter them?
Why or why not?

4. Do you consider obedience to God to be your
responsibility and a source of blessing? Why or why not?

5. Are you yielding to God's refining process in your life?
Allowing the trials of life to make you a better, not a
bitter, person?

Sum Up

Generational curses are a fact of life. Healthy families recognize them, confront them, and establish new patterns.
Forgiveness, patience, and love are crucial to this process.
Allowing the trials of life to bring us closer to God will
give us the transformation that we all desire. We may be a
broken people, but we do not serve a broken God.

Five

Moms Are Not Perfect: That Never Was the Goal

The search for identity and meaning is central to the human experience, and the need to count for something and to matter does not disappear when we become moms. Moms have a critically important role as the mentors of the next generation, but many of us struggle with feeling insecure in a world that values outward success and measures everything from looks to academics to material accomplishments. This is because the world gets caught up in tying identity to how well we "measure up." But if we as moms go down this path we will end up feeling insignificant and unsuccessful. Striving for self always ends up separating us not only from others but also from God. God wants us to enjoy the fruit of the work of our hands. But when measurements become idols we bow down and worship, we become their slaves. And slavery is never a happy state.

God's vision of motherhood does not include measurements because we have been made whole through Christ's sacrifice on the Cross. God created us to be ministers to our families, flowing out of our identity in Him. Satisfaction and joy come from embracing the importance of that ministry. However, we have to deal with the pervasive stress on moms to measure up to the world's standards. If we can get out from under the world's definition of success, we can stop being so anxious and truly appreciate who we are to our family.

One mom shared her redemptive story of constantly striving to live up to her family's expectations, as well as her own. Kelly is a beautiful, accomplished woman who was raised to be very much in control of her life. She trained as a doctor before she got married. She strove to be both attractive to the world and to achieve success in her professional life. These two elements, plus the ability to work hard to make the most of them, are what she had been taught from the time she was very young. Her parents had moved from Asia, and they had to work long hours to provide for the family. Kelly did her best not to squander her chance for success in the land of opportunity. Prior to becoming a mom, there seemed to be no challenge too difficult to navigate. She worked through every challenge, never allowing herself to give up.

Kelly and her husband decided together that she would take a hiatus from working to raise their children. Unexpectedly for Kelly, by having children some of her deepest insecurities surfaced. Kelly is a scientist, but there is no exact science to motherhood. The more she grew to love her children, the more she felt uncertain and even helpless in the face of the many demands of motherhood. She read many books on parenting and applied every mothering principle she could to her life.

She was very nervous about measuring up as a mom. This fear drove her to work even harder to be the "perfect mom." While working hard and doing a job well are good things, for Kelly, as for many moms, these goals can lead to a sense of unworthiness and guilt.

Kelly's anxiety increased, because no matter how early she woke up, one of her young kids was up before her. No matter how she tried to keep organized and on time, something would throw off her schedule. No matter how hard she tried to keep her home clean, the toys, laundry, and dirty dishes piled up. She could barely savor the many blessings of her family life because she was always worried that she would not be able to perform to perfection when the next demand surfaced. She knew that she could not continue this path of constant striving. Then God in His mercy gave Kelly a life-changing revelation.

One day as she was reading the Bible a verse jumped out at her: "The king's daughter is all glorious within" (Ps. 45:13 KJV). God does not require human perfection because we are seen through the perfection of Jesus. There is spiritual beauty that perhaps only Jesus can see; it has nothing to do with the world and is gained through a life committed to Jesus. Kelly realized she had been subconsciously using measurements to assure herself that she was doing a good job in all the spheres of her life, even in her spiritual life. Her strivings were actually blocking God's abundant grace in her life and only brought her fear.

Motherhood is not a performance through which we gain God's love and approval. We have been given both through Christ Jesus. God simply requires trust in Him to do what we are unable to do in our own striving. Kelly realized that she could continue to be a staff sergeant at home, demanding perfection, or she could show the same grace to her children that Jesus shows her. She does not want her children to be tormented with the same unattainable standards of excellence she was raised with. She does not want them to feel burdened with guilt if they fail, and she certainly does not want them to believe that they are only worthy of love if they are perfect. God has compassionately transformed Kelly through her struggles in motherhood.

MOMS AND MINISTRY

I, too, have struggled long and hard in the area of expectations. I have used measurements in my life, sometimes subconsciously, as a false mechanism to prove to myself that I am worthy. For me, it has been very important not to disappoint those I love, and while this at face value may seem like a good desire, in reality this fear is closely aligned to guilt and fear of failure. Motherhood, however, is not a performance but a ministry. Moms have a high calling, but we can see and embrace this vision only if we incorporate the knowledge that we are in a ministry free from any call to measure up.

Jesus does not want us to be our own harshest critic, tied ball and chain to the transitory values of this world or the need to measure up to loved ones' expectations. My illness has underscored the transitory nature of much of what I value. Educational and professional success, looks, social status, and popularity are all on my list of measurements. Interestingly enough, my severe illness has highlighted the fact that much of what I had measured myself against will not stand the test of time. However, what does stand the test of time is the love of my family and friends, all flowing from our heavenly Father. This ministry from my family has helped me not fall into depression concerning my present state of health.

One of the truly wonderful things about the eternal is that we don't have to worry that it will disappear. Everything God builds remains; what I build will die with me. God's call to me is to build as many eternal treasures as I will allow. Relationships built through prayer and unconditional love will form the most precious part of my legacy and ministry. His ministry through the Holy Spirit is to work in me and through me. Our Heavenly Father does not trample over us; we must freely give over to Him our hearts and lives.

I hope that you will not be stubborn like me and have to suffer a difficult challenge to recalibrate what you see as important. I was deeply concerned with how I was seen by the world, and this brought discontent and anxiety instead of peace and rest. My health crisis brought me to a standstill and this has been all to the good. In our ministry as moms, it is essential that we are at peace with who we are, not tormented with how we feel we are perceived by the world. God accepts us and we can have confidence in His acceptance.

The sense that I am not measuring up to my goals often gives me a sinking feeling that I am failing my family. But this feeling of judgment and fear does not come from the Lord; as the Lord said to Samuel in 1 Samuel 16:7: "People look at the outward appearance, but the LORD looks at the heart." God does not evaluate us through a series of benchmarks. We are to be ministers to our families and to live the life that has been marked out for us. God has given each of us various ministries and endeavors that only we can do, and one of the most important is ministering to our families. Our lives are not carbon copies but unique and individual, so comparisons to others are not valid in the kingdom of God.

Whether moms work exclusively in the home or also have a career outside the home, we all have to address the fact that the world wants to impose its measuring system on us. One of my friends recently told me she struggled to feel accepted in a playgroup because she felt overweight. This friend is lovely, but she does not feel that she is "skinny enough." So many of us glance at the mirror not feeling confident because we see "flaws" as defined by Hollywood and airbrushed magazine photos. Our heavenly Father cares about things like character, faith, hope, and love. These are the hidden things that God sees and our family feels emanating from us.

MOTHERHOOD IS NOT A COMPETITION

As twenty-first-century moms, we are participating in a culture with impossible expectations, and we have to fight the temptation to bring these expectations into our families. I grew up feeling that I was supposed to have high-level academic achievement, build a satisfying career, be a great wife, and at the same time raise high-achieving children. And the picture presented to the world has to look pretty. If we take on the world's measurements and aspirations, we will then take on the great weight of living up to those expectations. Most of us realize in our honest moments that we cannot come even close to achieving all of these worldly goals.

We are all doomed to sadness and emptiness if we continue to look for meaning in the world's measurements of success. This goes for men as well as women. Like the idols that captivated the Israelites in the Old Testament, the idols of today (money, status, prestige, and so on) are equally empty and unsatisfying in the end. According to the World Health Organization, use of antidepressant medication has skyrocketed an astonishing 400 percent since 1988 in America, much of it fueled by a sense of futility and emptiness in the land of plenty. Suicide rates have also had a shocking increase of 60 percent in the last fifty years, mostly in affluent countries such as ours.[1] We cannot ignore the fact that unhappiness and disappointment are tied into these depressing statistics. Unhappiness and disappointment that for all our ambition and striving, we are less satisfied and less happy.

Furthermore, we have to be aware of the fact that when we make the measurements of the world our idols, we are setting ourselves up in opposition to what God wants for us. God will not abide competitors (see the first, second, and third commandments in Exodus 20). He has put my husband and me through some very humbling experiences so that we would not march to the world's tune. He has also allowed us to experience some wonderful successes. The failures have been heartrending. They did get our attention in ways that success did not. Perhaps that is why we have experienced quite a few setbacks in our lives together. Through the failures, we finally realized that we both had a real problem with making idols of the world's measurements of success. I had hoped success would validate my identity, but like all idols, these idols ultimately failed me.

We can measure ourselves, and others, using various means. It could be some mental scorecard you use to check off a list of achievements: successful husband, great career, and accomplished kids. In Christian circles, the measuring up can comprise a different list: Where did your kid do missions work? Where are you or they volunteering? This "measuring up" list runs the gamut—human beings can use anything to establish perceived value. Most likely our measurements are tinged with our parents' voices.

But motherhood is in no way a competition. It is a ministry. We are not judged against each other. It is very clear that we should not measure others: "Do not judge, or you too will be judged" (Matt. 7:1). Jesus is warning us that God does not approve of us being in competition with others and making ourselves feel better by pointing out the failings of the competition. God does not operate in this fashion, and He wants us to be free of this toxic mind-set.

Fortunately, our heavenly Father does not judge any of us with these measurements. As a young mom I read the following passage: "There is neither Jew nor Gentile, neither slave nor free, nor is there male and female, for you are all one in Christ Jesus" (Gal. 3:28). These words transcend our thinking. Jesus does not want us to be defined by nationality, gender, and/or money. If we are concerned with these identity markers, we will be concerned with the measurements that are associated with them. As new creatures in Christ, we can live free from the fear that we are not valued, that we don't measure up. I cannot imagine my life as a homemaker and mom without the knowledge that I have value and meaning that exist beyond myself and my chores. The Lord is calling us to a different set of goals and aspirations as women and mothers.

MOTHERHOOD REQUIRES COURAGE

The word *ministry* in the Greek means "to serve." This is exactly what moms do. We minister to the emotional and physical needs of our families. We do so as God's ministers. There are no worldly measurements in the ministry of motherhood because it is not about external performance. If our heavenly Father cares not about the external but about the heart, this should be our perspective as well (1 Sam. 16:7). Jesus is not judging us, nor is He measuring us against each other. He is infusing us with His Holy Spirit to rise up daily and minister to our families. Because we don't have reviews and salary hikes to signify that we are doing our jobs well, motherhood requires a strong sense of mission and courage. Our ministry is to our husband and children and to our local community. Make no mistake: a stable, happy family is a tremendous blessing to any community. Many moms have to expand their vision of ministry to include not only what we do as mothers, but who we are in this world. As Jesus ministers to us and our families, we minister to them and to Him. This is true ministry.

Do not underestimate the impact of your ministry on the wider community. Moms are guides and mentors to the next generation, not only to our own children but through friendships, schools, and volunteering in this generation. We are raising kids who will greatly contribute to our society instead of being a drain on it. Our grandchildren and their grandchildren will benefit from what we are doing in and through our ministry today.

Valuing Motherhood

We moms have to face the fact that our culture undervalues motherhood. We have to make peace with this; otherwise we can feel judged as lacking worth and grow resentful as a result. Ann Crittenden's anecdote in her book, *The Price of Motherhood: Why the Most Important Job in the World Is Still the Least Valued*, underscores the continued devaluation of motherhood in our culture. Crittenden is a Pulitzer Prize–nominated writer for *The*

New York Times. She took an extended sabbatical from work to raise her son. At a cocktail party another guest accosted her and asked, "Didn't you used to be Ann Crittenden?"[2]

Many of us who choose to be stay-at-home moms have experienced this same sense of devaluation. So after a while it is easy to wonder if maybe our society is right. The Bible asks and answers the pertinent issue of value:

> Who can find a virtuous wife?
> For her worth is far above rubies.
> The heart of her husband safely trusts her. . . .
> She is not afraid. . . .
> She shall rejoice in time to come.
> She opens her mouth with wisdom,
> And on her tongue is the law of kindness. . . .
> Her children rise up and call her blessed. . . .
> Charm is deceitful and beauty is passing,
> But a woman who fears the LORD, she shall be praised.
> Give her of the fruit of her hands,
> And let her own works praise her in the gates.
> (Prov. 31:10–31 NKJV)

The above passage encompasses the life of a godly wife. Surprisingly, children are only mentioned once. This wife and mother is seen from the vantage point of her entire life and not just at a snapshot in time. God has a vision for our lives that is greater than ours. He deeply values our lives, and His plans for us do not stop at any one juncture. Now that I am in my fifties, I can grasp this important point. Jesus has many plans for me as a woman, but I have to be willing to give Him my trust to see the journey unfold. I also must surrender my own ambitions to take on His better plan for my life.

In the early years, motherhood is heavily weighted toward physical labor, but this decreases over time. As the kids grow, however, the requirements of mothering do not diminish. As Anne-Marie Slaughter famously wrote in her 2012 article in *The Atlantic*, "Why Women Still Can't Have it All," adolescents need their moms even more than they did when they were very young.[3] One of her teenage sons was struggling in a number of areas of his life. She was forced to reconsider her priorities and cut back for her family's benefit but to the detriment of her career. Slaughter writes, "Only when women wield power in sufficient numbers will we create a society that genuinely works for all women. That will be a society that works for everyone."[4] This article caused a maelstrom in the US, but Slaughter's argument is fundamentally flawed.

We see historically that there has been a tendency through-out the ages to equate unhappiness with a lack of empowerment and validation. For example, Karl Marx believed that only when the workers of the world united in power would it be possible for society to work for everyone. Millions were murdered in that attempt. Workers were certainly not happier in a workers' uto-pia. The truth is that unhappiness and discontent have existed from the beginning of human history because they are part of the human condition. As the serpent said to Eve, "Do I under-stand that God told you not to eat from any tree in the garden?" (Gen. 3:1). The power of jealousy and covetousness caused the peace and contentment that Adam and Eve experienced in the Garden to fly out the window, even though nothing externally had changed. In the end, Adam and Eve both sinned because they valued something more than their relationship with God.

As the story of the Garden of Eden demonstrates, given our human capacity for dissatisfaction, even perfect external circumstances do not guarantee long-term happiness. We have all seen good marriages with everything going for them break down from feelings of discontent. I call this the "I'm just not happy anymore" syndrome. The widespread prevalence of this problem tells us that Adam and Eve do in fact represent truth regarding human nature. We all have to deal with our own ability to screw things up even when everything is fine. We could have a great spouse, terrific kids, and fulfilling job and still be miserable. Adam and Eve had everything they needed, but they were easily swayed to dissatisfaction because they focused on the lack instead of the provision. I have been very good at focusing on the lack in my own life, but I am making concerted efforts to see the blessings of provision. My challenging health issues have brought a paradoxical healing into my emotional health because I can see what has remained in the wake of my illness.

A woman's continued inability to "have it all" is driving many women to distraction. The reality is no one can have it all. We have to remember Jesus did not come to "have it all." In fact, He upended humanity's take on power. Jesus came to serve and not be served, as He tells His disciples in Mark 10:43–45: "Whoever wants to become great among you must be your servant, and whoever wants to be first must be slave of all. For even the Son of Man did not come to be served, but to serve, and to give his life as a ransom for many." So we come back to the concept of service, of ministry. Few today are content to be humble and serve others; yet few people today seem truly happy. The sense of being cheated because we don't have it all reveals that our eyes are focused on the wrong prize.

GIVING THANKS AND PRAISE

The power of thanksgiving and praise brings with it transformation and renewal. In giving praise and thanks to our God, we put ourselves into the correct position in the universe. We may not measure up in the world's eyes, but that was never the right goal anyway. We can be confident that the God we serve obliterates all the worldly measures that we can think up. My favorite Christmas carol is "Joy to the World," and my favorite line is "He makes the nations prove . . ." In the end, He makes us worthy. We are not to prove ourselves worthy because we are not. We must take our eyes off of ourselves and put them firmly on Him.

As believers we can bless our Father with thanksgiving and praise. This pleases the heart of our Father and brings contentment to a dissatisfied soul. The Scriptures instruct us to be grateful. There are hundreds of verses, even whole psalms, dedicated to thanking God and reminding us of the importance of giving thanks. One of my favorites is "Give thanks in all circumstances; for this is God's will for you in Christ Jesus" (1 Thess. 5:18).

When you wake up in the morning, what are the first things that normally come to your mind? Too many mornings I admit that I wake up preoccupied with problems or worries. Usually I think about my busy schedule and what needs to get done. Other moms have different concerns: bills to be paid, a new car is needed, a child needs to go to the doctor, and so on. The Lord does not want us to start our day stressed. We can break this cycle by focusing on the Lord and giving thanks: "O God, You are my God; early will I seek You. . . . Give thanks to the LORD, for He is good; for His mercy endures forever. . . . Let the redeemed of the LORD say so" (Pss. 63:1; 106:1; 107:2 NKJV).

I have initiated the following routine to break this cycle of worry. Before I get out of bed, I thank God for the good things in my life. As soon as I am awake, I start thanking our heavenly Father for His many gifts. I try to take a few minutes out around noon to again consciously thank and praise our Father for His goodness to us. In the evening, before I go to sleep, I take time to thank Him again for the blessings of the day. I try not to take for granted everything He has given me. I naturally tend to look at the lack and forget His provision, just as Eve did. Giving thanks reorients me to the truth: I serve a God who has been abundantly gracious to me. I do not have to be afraid that He will withhold His goodness from me because He is disappointed in me.

Being grateful will help you deal more effectively with whatever situation you find yourself in. When we stop to count our blessings, we cannot help but be encouraged by what our heavenly Father has done. Encouragement also helps prepare us for what our heavenly Father wants to do for us going forward. We may still have challenges and difficulties before us, but giving thanks reminds us of all the Lord has already done for us. That encouragement can help us overcome the next challenges.

Cultivating gratitude in our lives for all the good things we have helps us establish the proper perspective on life. When we see more clearly, we can deal with problems more effectively (and even avoid some problems altogether!). Developing gratitude will also help you and your family combat the rampant materialism that is all around us. For if we want our children to develop an attitude of gratitude, they must see it in us first.

We are bombarded every day with the message that materialism is what matters. Everywhere we turn our culture is trying to sell us more stuff; the world wants us to believe that if we only bought this or used that, we would be happy. Of course, to get all that stuff the advertisers tell us we need, we have to work harder and longer. But this is contrary to God's economy. We can possess everything but be bankrupt in the Spirit. *Caveat emptor* is a Latin expression that means "buyer beware." We need to beware of what today's media are trying to sell us and our kids.

Because we are so exposed to materialism, our kids are in danger of growing up covetous and always wanting more things. Madison Avenue's bombarding us with advertisements every day doesn't help either. We are in danger of measuring ourselves in terms of what we own. Families may actually have a very good existence yet feel deprived because of society's "need" to possess more and more. Shopping has become a sport for many, including our young. Going to the mall is entertainment. Because credit is cheap, many youngsters, as well as oldsters, are in deep debt. Only by truly valuing the things of the Spirit can we combat this desire to value the material and find our self-worth in things.

One tangible way of showing our thanksgiving is by being generous to others. Most Christians have heard the verse "God loves a cheerful giver" (2 Cor. 9:7). We are called to bless others in His name. Giving to others allows us to be a blessing to them and to our heavenly Father. It is not by accident that the Lord promises in Matthew 7:2 that the measure you use for others will be the very same measure that God uses for you. When we give significantly of our material possessions, we set an example for our own children and help them develop a generous spirit as well. It is one of our greatest desires that our children are generous from their abundance, since it is clear that we serve an abundant God.

The Bible also says that "godliness with contentment is great gain" (1 Tim. 6:6). When we are free from the covetousness of the world, we will be content with what we are given. When we are free from striving after achievements, we will be content with who we are. God has given me what He wants me to have. God has made me to be who I am supposed to be. I am learning to be content through His reality.

Being so frail in my health and losing my looks to both age and facial nerve damage has taken me to places I never sought. My husband and children have been the outward evidence of God's love. They don't turn their eyes from me, they kiss and hug me, telling me I am beautiful, something that I perhaps once was but is now gone. My family's actions are a reflection of how God sees His daughters: "The king's daughter is all glorious within" (Ps. 45:13 KJV).

The Lord desires us to cease from striving to reach the impossible goals we have set for ourselves. He wants to replace worldly measures with the knowledge that He cherishes us as His daughters. I had to learn to look to Jesus and focus on being obedient to Him, knowing that is what brings Him pleasure. A humble, contrite heart is all that He requires. It is at the feet of Jesus I learned the peace that flows from a right relationship with God. I can cease from striving to be lovable, the greatest desire I had, because He loves His children unconditionally. It is a life-changing revelation to realize that I do not have to do anything to receive His love, nor do you.

As a minister of Christ to my family, I have embraced the fact that what I do reverberates through the generations and will have an impact on the lives of many, even after I am long gone. Whether this is for good or ill is within my grasp. I will have no other ministry that will have the same far-reaching impact.

Ponder

God's Word

Do not conform to the pattern of this world, but be transformed by the renewing of your mind. (Rom. 12:2)

People look at the outward appearance, but the LORD looks at the heart. (1 Sam. 16:7)

Your word is a lamp for my feet, a light on my path. (Ps. 119:105)

The Authors' Words

"The Lord desires us to cease from striving to reach the impossible goals we have set for ourselves. He wants to replace worldly measures with the knowledge that He cherishes us as His daughters."

Assess

1. List several standards by which you evaluate yourself and your children.
2. Where did these standards come from? Are they God's standards?
3. Are these standards hurting you or helping you? Are they hurting or helping your children?
4. "Few today are content to be humble and serve others; yet few people today seem truly happy." Do you agree? Do you believe these things are linked? Why or why not?

5. Have you ever felt that you "used to be" an accomplished person, but now you are "only a mom"? How do you counter that devaluing thought?

Sum Up

We seek measurements because we want to feel good about ourselves, ignoring the fact that these same measurements have the power to make us feel like failures in no one's eyes but our own. Our identities in Christ free us from judging ourselves according to worldly standards. He cherishes us, and He wants us to walk in His acceptance.

Six

Harvard Versus Heaven:
Start with Eternity in Mind

All moms need mentors. I am blessed to have an eighty-year-old woman in my life who generously shares her life and wisdom with me. When her son unexpectedly died, she said he was "honest and hardworking." Her words were powerful homage to her son's simple but good life. He was not the hero of his own story; he had lived a modest life of honor and dependability. When I die, I hope for such an epitaph because a crowded résumé and a list of worldly accomplishments cannot take the place of character and a life of faith.

It is easy to want it all for our kids; what is hard is raising them to be people of faith and character in an age of unbelief. The idols of this world—success, money, and looks—are often at odds with the spiritual destiny God has for our children. Too many of us make the mistake of believing otherwise. Gregory and I want our kids to live lives pleasing to God. Our heavenly

Father has a destiny for each of our children if only we surrender the worldly measurements we may have wanted for our children.

What we value is inextricably linked to what we envision for ourselves and our families. These days many moms have a litany of their children's accomplishments at the ready because this is what validates them as moms. In our quest to be seen as good mothers, we are vulnerable to wanting our kids to meet the world's expectations, whether or not they are appropriate. This is because we are prone to believe that having successful kids means we have been successful moms.

Jesus taught in the Gospels: "No one can serve two masters" (Matt. 6:24). My desire to raise high-achieving kids at times has been in tension with God's desire for them to be spiritually minded. It is hard not to be influenced by a society focused on churning out successful and accomplished children. Our kids are left in a very vulnerable position if we give into the world's idolatry of success. Don't get me wrong. It is a very good thing to raise children who work hard and work excellently; it is even better when they find deep satisfaction and fulfillment in what they are doing with their lives. But when they find their identities in these pursuits to the exclusion of their spiritual selves and their relationships with others, they are in for disappointment and discontent. The following story is only one of many I could have chosen to illustrate my point about the lengths our kids go to as they bow down to the world's idol of success.

A LOCAL SCANDAL

In 2009 there was a national scandal concerning academic cheating at our local high school in Hanover, New Hampshire. *The*

New York Times, People magazine, CNN, and Fox News made our town a local hangout for weeks since the scandal touched on the national obsession of getting our children into the best universities. Hanover is a well-to-do Ivy League town that takes academics very seriously. Students are expected to excel and go to prestigious colleges. Ivy League credentials rank as highly sought-after status symbols.

Just before finals, a group of students broke into the school and stole copies of the final exams. After an internal investigation, the police were brought in by the school administration, and they charged one student as the ringleader. The parents of the accused threatened lawsuits against the police and school and were able to get the charges significantly reduced. Many of the other students who participated but did not lead the cheating ring suffered much more serious consequences. The ringleader and his parents are Christians. They now find it difficult to interact with the local community because many believe the family's scholastic ambitions blinded their eyes for the need to take responsibility. Parents who subvert consequences also subvert character development in their children. And as the famous Greek philosopher Heraclitus famously said: character is destiny.

Our kids need to be raised with the knowledge that they are valuable whether they produce or not. God gives us His unconditional love; our love for our kids cannot be based on what they do, but who they are. Teenagers are often terribly insecure in a world that has such high aspirations. They are required to have great looks, great bodies, high test scores, and so on. When a child is insecure, loving and feeling loved is a tricky proposition. Wrong aspirations will cause our children to grow even more insecure, and they will look for love and affirmation in places that may be detrimental. If kids believe that their accomplishments determine their value, they will have a shaky sense of self-worth that will only grow shakier with the years.

Our goal for our children should be to discern over time what their true gifts are, not what we want them to be. This discernment in turn supports God's desire for them to be secure and mature adults, the very things they need to be able to create balanced and healthy lives in the future. We had three children in three and a half years, yet they are each beautifully unique. It would be foolish to have the same goals for each of our children. Gregory and I have tried to focus on character development in an age-appropriate context. This takes time and comes with disappointments. But if you persevere in this effort, you will see great fruit over time. We have to remember that youngsters are exactly that, young. They need to be given time, and lots of it, to grasp wisdom.

We seem as a society to be very adept at raising kids who remain kids. Eternal adolescence is a bane of modern society. Men and women experiencing a midlife crisis is in many ways a replication of teenage angst. Fifty-year-old women who dress like twenty-year-olds are a disheartening modern-day phenomenon, and men who leave wives of thirty years for much younger women is a sad everyday occurrence. Our culture worships youth to such an extent that age is no barrier to childish behavior. The solution to this is to make sure we are growing in maturity and embracing wisdom as the years pass.

For our children, the solution is to allow them to grow up by taking on the responsibilities that come with age. Shielding adult children from reality is not doing them a favor. For example, allowing adult children to live rent-free at home is not helping anyone, least of all them. The same principle is true for our younger children. We must allow them to understand that as they grow, so will their responsibilities in life. Helping at home on a regular basis, summer jobs, doing their tasks well should be expected. The wisdom our children learn by understanding that their actions have consequences will be invaluable as they become adults. Those consequences, whether good or bad, must be felt to have any impact. Shielding our children from the negative consequences of their actions only makes them more likely to repeat those actions. None of us wants to see our kids become lifelong adolescents.

LOVING OUR CHILDREN
THROUGH THEIR JOURNEY

Recently I had a call from a friend with whom I had not spoken for some time. Barbara wanted to know how my health was progressing. Toward the end of the phone conversation, she brought up her son. She sounded tired as she talked. Stevie is a very nice kid. She and her husband have poured their lives out for him, but nothing has turned out the way she had expected. Even though Stevie is a good student, he did not do well enough in high school to be admitted to a top university. Instead, he graduated from a less rigorous college, and he has found it difficult to start a career. She ended her story by saying, "I am at the point of asking, was all the sacrifice worth it?" For Barbara the time, effort, and expense now seem unnecessary since the results have not met expectations. Barbara had cut her workload in half to raise her son, and this resulted in a career that had not met expectations.

The sacrifices they made, the years they poured into their child, have now left the couple with a hollow feeling. Disappointment is at the end of misguided aspirations; we have to be sure that our hopes and dreams for our children are for heaven, not Harvard. My own belief is that love is never wasted; it is never a mistake. I am sure that Barbara has not made a mistake pouring her life out for her son and family, and in time she will realize that the love she poured into her son has made him the kind, caring person he is. So often we take what we have for granted, focused on what we don't have.

What is a mistake is for parents to take on the world's measurements of success and then use these to validate the success of our children and our parenting. The Lord does not make mistakes with creating our kids just the way they are. They are "fearfully and wonderfully made" (Ps. 139:14). Just as moms are not measured and found wanting by God, our children are not to be judged by the world's standards. Jesus has a higher goal than anything we could want for our children. This goal is beyond the worldly ambitions for money, fame, or power—none of which is eternal. God is calling our kids to be consecrated to Him. As moms, worldly measures of success can be a true enemy. Dashed expectations often trigger emotional upheavals and disappointments; but in reality, we may have chosen the wrong direction for our children to begin with.

Moms have to know that our heavenly Father is with our children and is guiding them. We have to surrender our expectations for them because our worldly dreams simply may not be in line with God's will for our children. Regret does not come because God failed our children; rather, it enters when our aspirations are tied to the world's definitions of success. God loves our children more than we do. Meditate on this and your perspective will change forever. Understanding the certainty of His love for our children and His life path for them has given us the strength to allow God to unfold His plan in our children.

I was opposed to our daughter Sasha going into the US Army after graduating from Dartmouth, although Gregory was not. In prayer, I felt strongly that she was answering God's call. I also recognized that I needed to respect her choices as an adult. My role now is to support our adult daughter through prayer and any counsel she may request. Eventually each of our children has to make his or her own way in life, not anxious about pleasing earthly parents. This is what we all want for our kids. We are raising them to be adults who are confident and responsible in their decision making.

Gregory and I want our children to work hard and to work excellently. There is an inherent tension with instilling life skills while simultaneously instilling in our children the sure knowledge they are loved unconditionally. I have been guilty of sending mixed signals: "Work harder and don't make me send you back to the computer to do a better job" can sound like, "You had better get an A, or I will be disappointed in you." Learning to work well is an important life skill and there is no substitute for it. Communication with children has to be nuanced so they don't feel condemnation, especially as they grow older. This is at times difficult I must admit, given my human nature and the fact that I do grow weary repeating the same message over and over. This is where the 10 to 1 rule comes in: ten parts love, affirmation, and reinforcement for every one part constructive criticism. Use that ratio, or anything close to it, and you won't go wrong.

BEING A STUDENT OF YOUR CHILDREN

My husband and I have tried to be students of our children. Time is crucial in this endeavor because it has allowed our children's characters, dreams, and weaknesses to unfold before us. We have had many occasions to recalibrate our parenting to meet our children's needs. It is only in close observation that we can help our children discover the special gifts they have been given. Ultimately, we want our children to follow God's high calling.

Recently our eldest son had to make a difficult decision, and Gregory and I offered him different advice. This happens to all couples, and it is critical for Gregory and me to show each other respect while disagreeing. Life is complicated, and there are times when the way forward feels mysterious and even scary. To be honest, I am unsure that our son has chosen the best path even though what I counseled is what he has decided to do. We are called to live a life of faith dependent on God to bring His purposes to pass and trusting in His guidance and goodness. There is no substitute for trust in the life of faith.

It is in discerning our children's strengths and weaknesses, their likes and dislikes, that we as parents can best help our children set good and reasonable goals. Gregory and I don't believe that getting our kids into elite universities necessarily makes us good parents. Plenty of terrible parents have gotten their kids into great schools. Many parents stress about academic achievement because our society views it as the gateway to great jobs and careers. But entrance into even the most elite universities will not help the young person who is untrustworthy, uncaring, and uncouth. Character does determine destiny in the long run. We as parents have to keep our eyes focused on that reality.

Parental dreams run the gamut; your dream for your child may be professional sports or music or acting. These pursuits just may not work beyond a certain level. Naturally the discipline and training required by sports or musical pursuits will not go to waste. But if our children tie our unrealistic parental expectations to how they value themselves, our kids will experience bitterness. Our children are not created to fulfill our dreams. My mom tried to live vicariously through me, and I could not trust her to have my best interests at heart. Gregory and I believe we can best help our kids by discovering who God has made them to be. We don't want their lives to be one big letdown because they didn't meet our unrealistic expectations. If we want our children to be businessmen when they are gifted to be pastors, or if we want our kids to be doctors when they have the attributes and desire to be outstanding teachers, we will be doing them a great disservice.

It is easy to be overly influenced by those around us ("our neighbor's kid went to Yale, and he's no smarter than our son") or family traditions ("we've always been lawyers/pastors/teachers in this family") or our own fears for the future ("if our child doesn't get into this school he won't get a good job"). Comparing our children to others is always a bad idea. Comparing them to grandparents or other family members is little better. While we probably won't be able to totally block out these influences, our child's future should be determined by who he or she really is.

Parents have to allow the Holy Spirit to direct us in discerning what is best for our kids. Children approach life differently. Gregory and I can observe this truth in our own family. While our children share important similarities, it is clear that genetics only goes so far. Each of our children has needed a different approach from the time they were very young. In fact, some of our most serious parenting mistakes were made trying to apply a one-size-fits-all approach early in our family life.

CONSEQUENCES OF SUPER-HIGH-PRESSURE PARENTING

A super-high-pressure approach to parenting is popular in some circles, and because it seems to yield certain results, it is currently the flavor of the month. Some call it the "tiger mom" approach. This type of parenting is tied to the world's way of measuring performance and success. In reality, many kids wilt under this approach and suffer greatly from performance anxiety and fear of failure. Boys are different than girls, and they receive parental guidance differently. I can guarantee that a "tiger mom" style would not have worked with my sons. My husband and I personally know a number of kids (especially boys) who have been deeply scarred by "tiger moms."

My daughter, who thrives on achievement, would have turned bitter with such an approach. Sasha wants love and support from Gregory and me, and she is extremely sensitive to what she perceives as our judgment and condemnation. Being a "tiger mom" would have turned our mother-daughter relationship sour. Sasha and I struggled for five years over my desire for her to play the piano. I finally realized that the cost was not worth the accomplishment. I gave up my dreams of her being a pianist because I saw her flourish in other endeavors she enjoys. I am really happy I surrendered because it restored peace to our family's nightly routine. Sasha turned to singing, her true talent, for artistic fulfillment.

Our boys have required more accountability because they have a "live for the moment" attitude—as many boys, and young men, do. Gregory and I have a 10 to 1 rule: ten parts love, encouragement, and support for every one part discipline. So while we are calling them to be accountable for homework and chores, we are careful not to break their spirits in the pursuit of academics. Our children need our help and encouragement to discover their own special mix of gifts. They need us to have grace for them and to help them develop those abilities.

SCHOOLING: MAKING WISE CHOICES

Using schooling as an effective and edifying part of our children's development is as crucial to us as it is for any parent. But our ultimate goal for all our children is heaven, not Harvard. Education in the twenty-first century is an adventure that requires courage and wisdom. My parents' schooling decisions were typical of their time and socioeconomic class. They chose a town in New Jersey that had a solid reputation for public schools, and they never had a moment's doubt or cause to reconsider. My educational course was set before I turned five, and I was on autopilot until college applications. The path of my parents' generation, at least that of middle-class America, was relatively clear and straightforward.

Parents today have something that our parents did not: choice. This choice has evolved due to a number of factors, the most important of which I believe is parents' justifiable displeasure at what is occurring in many classrooms. Ultimately, we have to consider what is best for our children and our families as we wade through the options of public schools, charter schools, magnet schools, Christian schools, private schools, and home-schooling. The plethora of choice can be confusing, but as we observe our children and their learning styles and as we come to know the school options available to our families, the way does become clearer.

My husband and I were intimidated by choices we faced as parents when we began the process of school selection. After a combined total of over fifty years of schooling with our four children, we view all these choices as legitimate. Making the best choice for your child depends on a number of important factors. The overriding factor is what will be the best learning environment (academically, morally, and socially) for your child. To understand that, you must truly understand your child.

In our family we have chosen Christian schools, public schools (in different states), private schools (again in different states plus two foreign countries), and homeschooling with two different children. In effect, we have done it all. We did not choose this path because we are hard to please or were looking for the next hot trend. In fact, my father always said that children need routine and stability. I agree wholeheartedly; but when educational situations don't work, it is important to have the courage to change course if need be. We have learned to pray over each child and ask for direction for the coming year. Assumptions that one way of schooling is the only way are no longer viable. We have to be on top of schools and be willing to hear God if we have to recalibrate our child's school path.

For example, in fourth grade our Daniel was mercilessly bullied at a private school in Bermuda. Verbal abuse, pushing, and shoving were daily problems. The guidance counselors simply put their hands up in defeat and the headmaster did nothing to help. This was supposed to be the best school in Bermuda. Daniel is an interesting mix of charm and stoicism, so at first he did not complain. One day he revealed that school was becoming untenable for him. We did our best to get the school's professionals involved, but they didn't do anything. After much prayer and conversation, we pulled Daniel out of school and began to homeschool.

I had never felt called to homeschool. I have no pedagogical or philosophical reservations regarding homeschooling; I just did not think I could be successful at it. Understanding who you are as a mom and knowing your limitations are key. Early in the 1990s, I knew a family where the mom's health was quite fragile. She still tried to homeschool, and it did not work. When the mom was too tired to teach, she simply didn't. This particular situation did not end well. On the other hand, I have seen families do incredible things through homeschooling and have really admired these families for their dedication. An honest assessment of one's strengths and limitations is crucial for success. Don't homeschool just because you think you should or because everyone in your community is doing it. It is a huge commitment and requires enormous self-discipline to do well. On the other hand, don't reject homeschooling because it feels foreign and intimidating.

Schools are a tricky proposition these days for parents and kids. We need to consider this reality: if an adult does not like her environment, if she is not happy with her workplace, or if she decides what her peers are doing is morally unacceptable, she can leave. All too often we throw our kids into untenable situations and the message to our kids is: make it work! While some might quibble with my assertion that we have the freedom to move on from difficult professional situations (bills need to be paid), the reality is that we can find other jobs—perhaps with difficulty, but we can still do it—and we can set boundaries with the dysfunctional people in our workplaces. Our kids cannot just walk out of negative school situations. So if we don't do our due diligence as parents, we could be leaving our kids in situations where they are bullied, abused, and even worse.

We homeschooled Daniel for six months. I tailored the schedule to Daniel. Studies have shown that kids do better at school with a late start time, but most schools start early because it is easier for working parents. But what is difficult for schools is easily arranged at home. So we set up a daily routine of physical exercise from 9 to 9:30 a.m. He could swim in our pool and take a run around the neighborhood. This really woke him up since he loves to sleep in the morning. Daniel met me at 9:30 in the dining room, and we began the day with English. In the course of six months, we read some of the world's greatest short stories. It was a revelation to Daniel, who was convinced he did not enjoy reading. His favorite story was "The Death of Ivan Ilych" by Leo Tolstoy. Years later, Daniel still refers to it. Daniel wrote his best essay on this story, and it was in those months he became a dedicated reader.

Daniel's favorite lesson of the day was biblical ethics. This was where he really came alive. I look back at these six months as some of my most enjoyable with Daniel. Gregory taught him French and math. Daniel was able to make great strides because he was held accountable and it was at his pace and level. Immediate, constructive feedback is key to academic success. That's something that no teacher in a class of twenty-five-plus students can consistently provide, no matter how great a teacher he or she is.

We were put in the challenging position of homeschooling our eldest son in high school after our return from Bermuda. We could not be sure of the outcome, but we knew Christian in his first month of American high school was not flourishing. His success in the first two years of the British high school system in Bermuda didn't translate well to America. We could not allow his last two years at high school to be a nightmare through no fault of his own. So we built what was effectively an independent study program for him. Mentoring from a family that had homeschooled for years was key to our success. They advised us to build a curriculum that would show excellence as we began the process of college applications. Clear goals while homeschooling are essential. Christian is now a senior at a fine Ivy League school. God's grace indeed.

EMBRACING FAILURE

Teaching your child how to deal with failure will be richly rewarded in your child's life. A fear of failure has been hugely toxic for many of us. It only brings disappointment and bitterness with it. We have to embrace God's view of this world and know that failure is simply part of the human equation. While this is counterintuitive, as well as countercultural, we need to learn how to embrace failure and to teach our children to do the same. Embracing failure, learning from it, and bringing it to God so that He can redeem it is very powerful spiritually.

I myself have lived through many failures. Some of these failures I experienced as a professional woman, and some as a mom. My husband has an impeccable academic record, and after graduating from Harvard Business School, we lived in Paris, New

York, and Buenos Aires. He was recruited to Silicon Valley, where he rose to become the CEO of a successful dot-com startup. My husband was on the cover of *Time* magazine and Po Bronson devoted a chapter in his New York Times bestseller *The Nudist on the Late Shift* to my husband's gung ho work style and success.[1] Things seemed to be rolling in our lives. Then the dot-com crash came. We were grateful that Gregory wasn't fired, sued, or jailed like many of his peers, but they certainly were painful years.

It was our faith in a good Father that allowed us to get through this very difficult period of public failure. It took time, of course. Dead and dying dreams are hard. But now when Gregory talks about the realities of success and failure to our own children or to Harvard Business School students, they pay attention. When our kids come to us for advice, they know that our wisdom is based on hard-earned experience. Young adults must learn that life is humbling and that failure is part of the process.

Gregory talks profoundly of failure when what all his MBA students expect to hear about is a route to guaranteed success. My children listen to me when I say, "Don't give up and don't give in." They have seen us walking the talk. I am seeing real courage and determination develop in our kids. Even a significant failure can draw us into a more profound, compassionate understanding of life and a more accurate understanding of ourselves if we take the time to learn the lessons our heavenly Father has for us in our failures.

If you teach your children to embrace failure and not to be afraid of its consequences, you will be unleashing a freedom and a creativity that will bring their own joy. Your kids will not be afraid to try new things and be adventurous in life. If our kids are afraid of failure, it is because they have the expectation of being measured harshly. They simply will not want to venture outside the box. Even if they do find the courage to explore new things, they will still be stifled by performance anxiety. Life is not a performance. Life is an opportunity to be truly present in God's world, to find deep meaning and joy in whatever He has created us to do. Some failures are part of God's plan for us because He knows there are certain deep truths that we simply cannot master via success.

Bad things can happen if we do not teach our children to handle the stress of failure. On December 16, 2013, my husband went to Harvard University for a business meeting. It was early in the morning, and he was startled by police denying him entrance to Harvard Yard. Harvard University was in lockdown due to bomb threats from an unknown source. Gregory was accosted by journalists asking his opinion about the dangerous situation. The incident at Harvard made international headlines. We later learned that the threat was in fact nonexistent. The FBI traced the threatening e-mails to a Harvard student. Twenty-year-old Eldo Kim had concocted a bizarre plan to get out of final exams. He had sent e-mails to Harvard authorities alerting them to the fact that bombs had been placed in various buildings across the campus. In the e-mails, Kim wrote ominously that they had better "be quick for they will go off soon."[2] Fortunately it was a hoax, but Kim is facing the full consequences of his actions: he was caught, expelled from Harvard, and is now facing jail time.

On college campuses across our country, more students are resorting to extreme measures to deal with the stress of trying to get the best grades. The same article in the *Huffington Post* puts it bluntly: "Experts say that students' mental health is increasingly becoming a focal point on college campuses."[3] An increasing number of kids are arriving on campus with mental health issues, and a psychologist recently warned the American Psychological Association that "it's hard [for counseling centers] to keep up with the numbers of students coming in."[4] Josh Gunn, president of the American Counseling Association was quoted as saying, "You frequently hear those who work in higher education talk about the perception that students are coming to campus with fewer coping resources. You couple the fewer coping resources with the increased pressures and expectations that are placed on students, and it's not all that surprising that the occasional student resorts to some form of extreme measure such as this."[5]

Our kids are growing up with much more material wealth than we had. As my mother pointed out, in the 1960s and '70s even if a family had money there was simply less to buy. She said this as we were in a McDonald's line watching the kids open the free toys that came with the Happy Meals. Everywhere kids go now, material things are handed out: goody bags, free stuff at sports events, and so on. Material wealth does not equip kids to handle the realities of life. We have to help our children develop a realistic view of life. I graduated from college in the 1980s in the face of a tough economy. My generation was raised to figure out how to build our lives the best we could. We expected to struggle for a job. We were ambitious, but it was not at the mythic level that it is today for many parents and their kids. I was not afraid that one failure would ruin my life. College was seen as an important key to my success, but it was not the idol upon which all my dreams would be made or broken.

This freedom to embrace failure and not be fearful of the future is being denied to many of our young. Kids are turning to cheating, to performance-enhancing drugs, and to other strategies because they are afraid of failure. They are afraid they are not measuring up. God wants our homes to be bastions of His love and guidance, not judgment and condemnation if the "performance" does not meet expectations. Let us moms be students of our children to understand the unique human beings our heavenly Father has made them to be and allow His Holy Spirit to guide us in raising them.

Ponder

God's Word

Do not think of yourself more highly than you ought, but rather think of yourself with sober judgment, in accordance with the faith God has distributed to each of you. For just as each of us has one body with many members, and these members do not all have the same function, so in Christ we, though many, form one body, and each member belongs to all the others. We have different gifts, according to the grace given to each of us. (Rom. 12:3–6)

I praise you because I am fearfully and wonderfully made. (Ps. 139:14)

But the goal of our instruction is love from a pure heart and a good conscience and a sincere faith. (1 Tim. 1:5 NASB)

The Authors' Words

"Our goal for our children should be to discern over time what their true gifts are, not what we want them to be. This discernment in turn supports God's desire for them to be secure and mature adults, the very things they need to be able to create balanced and healthy lives in the future."

Assess

1. Have you as a parent used the world's measurements of success to validate the success of your own parenting?

2. Parenting from fear is self-defeating. What other parental motivators are self-defeating? Which ones are problems for you?
3. If success and accomplishment are not the ultimate goals, what are?
4. Do you believe this: "If you teach your children to embrace failure and not to be afraid of its consequences, you will be unleashing a freedom and a creativity that will bring their own joy"? Why or why not?
5. Do you believe that God loves your children more than you do and that you can trust God with your children?

Sum Up

Life is an opportunity to be truly present in God's world, to find deep meaning and joy in whatever He has created us to do. Failures are part of God's plan for us because He knows there are certain deep truths that we simply cannot master via success. Raising our kids to embrace life in its totality will free them from fear, something we all want for our kids.

Seven

Sex, Drugs, and Rock and Roll: Answering Tough Questions

A few years back, Tyler Charles wrote a much-quoted article for *Relevant* magazine entitled "Almost Everyone is Doing It: A surprising new study shows Christians are having premarital sex and abortions as much (or more) than non-Christians."[1] In the opening paragraph, Charles writes that 80 percent of young unmarried Christians have had sex and that two-thirds have been sexually active in the last year. You may be like me, hesitant to believe statistics because they can be so easily manipulated. But whether these statistics are exactly right or off by 30 percent is beside the point. No matter what, these are scary numbers for parents. They are reflective of the battle that we face today, even within the church. All too often Christian parents raise their children in a bubble, trying to protect them from everything. Frequently this bubble collapses in the face of the real world. Ignoring the real world is a mom's first mistake. Our second mistake is that we often unknowingly become conformed to this world.

Counteracting today's dominant cultural winds is an uphill battle, even for the strongest of families. In this chapter we want to tackle some of the hardest issues facing moms today. We are going to look at how we can deal with a host of specific challenges and temptations that our children face. At the same time we will explore how we can establish godly patterns that will help our children stand strong against the prevailing cultural forces.

PRAY WITHOUT CEASING

"Rejoice always, pray without ceasing, in everything give thanks; for this is the will of God in Christ Jesus for you" (1 Thess. 5:16–18 NKJV). When I keep my eyes open to what my kids are doing and I am connected to God in intercession for them, I am reminded of this important truth: no matter how much I love my kids, Jesus loves them even more. He is seated at the right hand of the Father making intercession for them. That's right: Jesus Himself is praying for us and our families even as I am writing this sentence and you are reading this book. And He wants us to be doing the same thing.

I believe that I cannot pray enough during the day: for myself, my family, and for the wider community. "Pray without ceasing" means that when I am driving the car instead of listening to music, my time is better spent in prayer. I have joined every prayer group available to me, and I have created prayer groups when there were none available. I pray at night and during the day, with my husband and my children. Prayer is the most important spiritual weapon moms have because it puts us in direct communication with Jesus.

Gregory and I pray all the time that if our children are up to something that we are the *first*, not the *last* to know. God has answered this prayer many times, even when both the reality and the consequences have been unpleasant. God has moved in so many ways in our marriage and in our children through prayer. To be honest, our four children range in the faith spectrum, but when times get tough they all turn to their loving Father in prayer.

Gregory and I began praying for our children while they were in the womb, and we are now praying for their futures. I cannot wait to meet their future spouses for whom I have prayed for over two decades. My daughter has said it will be a grave responsibility to bring home her intended husband because of our prayers. This is all to the good.

THE NECESSITY OF UNDERSTANDING CHRISTIAN HISTORY

We are raising children in a world that mocks the concepts we are trying to teach them. Sadly, being a Christian is not seen as cool in many parts of our society. This makes it doubly important for our children to know that they are part of a vital, dynamic faith that has changed the world for the good over the course of thousands of years. Do not underestimate the impact the cultural elites' disdain for our faith has on our children. It pervades almost every aspect of media and academia today. Frankly, this has been a struggle in our own family since our kids want to be seen as sophisticated and cool, part of the "in" crowd.

Children in particular want to be part of a club, and this is because we all want to belong to something greater than ourselves. Christian parents need to make sure that our children are not ashamed of the faith. In order to embrace Christianity, they must be proud of it. Fortunately there is a great deal to be proud of. No matter what the world is saying about our faith, our kids have to be confident that Christianity is worthy of their lives. This starts, of course, with their being in a real relationship with Jesus, but it includes understanding at least some of the many great things Christians have done for our world. It is not by accident that our faith is the largest and fastest-growing in the world.

Christianity has been the impetus for many of the most important cultural advances in history, whether it was the abolition of the slave trade, the establishment of universal suffrage and the modern legal system ("equal justice for all" comes directly from the biblical concept that we are all equal in God's eyes), or the idea that the rich have a responsibility to help the poor (from Jesus' words, "to whom much is given, from him much will be required" [Luke 12:48 NKJV], as well as many other biblical passages). Christians were the force behind the greatest explosion of literacy in the world. Christians want everyone to be able to read the Scriptures and have advocated for universal education as a result. Some of America's greatest leaders, such as Abraham Lincoln, learned how to read by reading the Bible. In these ways and countless others, Christ's church has been a strong force for good in our world for two thousand years.

Ironically we live in a time when tolerance is seen as the supreme good, except when it comes to matters of the Christian faith. There exists a paradoxical tendency within this worldview to mock and disdain those who are Christians. One of my children recently said at the dinner table that at his public school every religion is accepted except Christianity. It is not "cool" to be a Christian these days, and as parents we have to counteract this by educating our kids in the great history of the faith. Kids who are embarrassed by their faith in the wake of increasing mockery and intolerance will find reasons to walk away from it. As parents, we have to make it a practice to instruct our children not only in the Scriptures but also in the admirable history of our faith.

This is not to deny that there have been many failings throughout church history. Yet we cannot blame Christ for the failings of individual Christians. Failings must be laid at the feet of humankind, not the Creator. This is the essence of the gospel: we all need a Savior. The minister who fails to heed wise counsel or the church leader who commits adultery needs a Savior just as much as any one of us. Help your kids to understand that Christianity encompasses over two billion people. In any group that size there are going to be exceptions to the rule. We can point to the many accomplishments of His followers: from Mother Teresa to Thomas Aquinas to Corrie ten Boom to Martin Luther King Jr. to Billy Graham. These individuals stand as powerful testimony to the incredible impact for the good our faith has had over the centuries.

Nicholas, our youngest, has shown great courage in sharing and defending his faith. At the end of his fifth grade graduation ceremony, each of the hundred or so kids was asked to come to the microphone and share his or her career goal. In our Ivy League town there was a predictable pattern of career aspirations: doctor, architect, writer, teacher, and so on. Nicky was one of the last to speak and the gasp was audible when he said, "I want to be a Christian missionary to Asia." We want our children to have a strong inner core—they need to know what they believe and why. We must help them in this, but their own relationship with God will be the bedrock upon which their faith is built.

One of the many deep truths of the Bible is that if we accept the ways of this world we (and our children) will eventually take on its characteristics. Over time we will be conformed to its prevailing modes of behavior if we do not actively incorporate biblical truths into our lives. Only in establishing a relationship with Jesus will our children choose the Lord's way, because it is far less sensually appealing than the life of sex, drugs, and rock and roll. We know that our heavenly Father does not want us not to be conformed into the world's mold. Instead, our Father wants us to be "transformed by the renewing of your mind" (Rom. 12:2).

SEX

Our society's view of sex is deeply flawed and wounding. One reason is our culture's idolatry of romantic love. Many of us see romantic love as the great quest of our lives. Though in prior centuries divine love, or *agape*, was seen as the highest and best example of true love, many now look to *eros* (romantic or sexual love) for their fulfillment. Our culture propagates the belief that romantic love should be the most satisfying relationship in our lives. When we don't "find" it, we are left disappointed and dissatisfied.

I can relate to this truth because, for many years, romantic love was my answer to my wounded identity. But instead of my dream, I found a human. More than a few of us come to our marriages with unrealistic expectations. We are fed by media-driven images of everlasting love, but invariably the tensions of real life pull people apart. What help keep a couple together and build a happy family life are not only romantic love but mutual respect, friendship, good communication, and a vision for something beyond themselves.

We experience transcendence through our relationship with God. Our relationship with our eternal Father gives us the source of ongoing commitment and love that we are longing for. This commitment must be modeled for our kids for, as we all know in child rearing, more is caught than is taught. If our own marriage is an example of walking together with love, respect, and lots of forgiveness, we will be making our children's future path easier.

Many young women, through Facebook, Instagram, and other social media, are posting lewd pictures in order to draw attention to themselves. Women now find themselves complicit in an objectifying process as old as time. Lena Dunham is the main actress and writer of the HBO show *Girls*. This show, and many like it, portrays sex stripped of any deep connectedness to another human being and sex becomes trivialized for mere entertainment value. *Girls*, like many current TV shows and movies, mirrors a generation of young adults who are turning sex into demeaning expressions of physicality which in turn promotes the continued objectification of women.

The women on this show are referred to as "girls." Twenty-six is still a girl? One of the tasks of any family is to raise children who embrace maturity and the wisdom that experience brings. Dunham was recently asked why she was randomly naked so much on the show.[2] She answered, "If you are not into me, that's your problem, and you are going to have to work that out with whatever professionals you've hired." The message here is that sex sells, so women should be participating in order to profit from it. Sadly, this cultural trend will grow worse with time because so much money is being made from it. Taste levels are pushed ever lower in order to titillate an increasingly shock-proofed audience.

So how do we raise both boys and girls who will not devalue sex? Our children must know who they are and what they believe. This is because we live in a culture that preaches tolerance but is intolerant of high moral standards. The cultural elite often ridicules virtue as old-fashioned and unnecessary. At home, moms and dads who model faithfulness and respect will make it much easier for their children to see the blessings that come from a strong married life. Respect is an essential ingredient to the importance of valuing sex. If children see their parents respecting the Lord, respecting one another, and making wise decisions for their families, then they will experience the blessings that flow out of such a relationship. Our children will want such a relationship for themselves as adults. They will also be equipped with the building blocks to build their own functioning, loving family.

Our children's friends are an integral part of their lives. "Bad company corrupts good character" highlights the importance of sound friendships (1 Cor. 15:33). Children are survivors, at least in the short term. If they are thrown in a bad situation, they will try to make it work. Adults can choose friends, but kids are consigned to their neighborhoods and schools. Children want friends, they want community, and they want to be popular. Sometimes because they are afraid or lack confidence, they don't make the right choices regarding friends. Kids find it much easier to make good choices in life if their peers are making wise choices. This is an obvious point, but an important one.

If your children have friends who are dragging them down, as a mom you may be required to make dramatic decisions—such as putting your children in a different school, or perhaps even choosing to homeschool. Our family was put in this position, and we are happy that we did not passively just hope for the best. Hoping rarely gets you where you need to go.

DATING AND OUR CHILDREN

This is an area that can be justifiably intimidating to parents. Dating in my generation began in high school, but now it often starts in middle school. This is true of many of the issues confronting our kids. They have to deal with sensitive areas of life at a much younger age than prior generations. Obviously twelve- and thirteen-year-olds are more vulnerable than kids in high school, which is why we did not allow our children to date in middle school. Only in high school did we begin to allow closely supervised dating. True, this did not make us super popular with some of our kids for a period of time. But remember: we are not called to be popular with our children; we are called to be their parents.

Sexual standards have to be addressed by parents at an earlier age because of the sexualized nature of our culture. We cannot allow the world to dictate to us and mold our standards. The world's standards are pressing in where we least expect it as parents. Gregory and I try to be careful about the TV shows and movies our kids watch. This on occasion has caused problems with other parents who seem to think that anything on five-hundred-plus channels is just fine for a ten-year-old. We are vigilant about the increasingly sexualized curriculum content at school. We read everything that comes our way, and we show up to parents' informational meetings. We have learned to not shy away from confronting policies that infringe on our parental responsibilities.

We as parents have to be the ones who give our kids enough information about the reality of life in an age-appropriate and godly way. Do not shy away from this area of life, because the world does not shy away from it. We must communicate with our children about dating and the decision to be pure from an early age, even though this is going to lead to some difficult conversations. Then we cannot stop communicating with our children on these subjects. We are swimming upstream on virtually all of these issues; we must continue to communicate the sound biblical and scientific basis for our convictions.

If our daughters have a strong and healthy bond with their dads, then they will seek to replicate that with their potential mates. And if the parents show deep respect toward each other and value the physical and emotional connections in their relationship, then they will pass on terrific generational role models to their kids. This will go a long way to counteract the prevailing cultural winds.

DRUGS

Nigella Lawson is a successful cookbook author and TV hostess. Her divorce made international headlines because she was married to a billionaire who alleged that her loose behavior was having a terrible effect on both her children and his children from their first marriages. In the divorce proceedings, Lawson admitted to not only leaving drugs around the home for their teenagers to use, but she also admitted to partaking of the drugs with her kids and their friends. Lawson says she loves her kids, but we are reminded of the truth in Galatians 6:7 that we all eventually reap what we sow.

Our family has lived amid extreme affluence in New York City, Silicon Valley, Washington, and Bermuda. Drug use is as rampant in wealthy California and Bermuda as it is in the relatively impoverished Vermont–New Hampshire area. In fact, Vermont and New Hampshire have the highest use of drugs among its young in the nation.

Universities don't publicize it, but many students today are self-medicating in order to get themselves through exams. Adderall and Resveratrol are ubiquitous on many campuses. Students freely use them to pull all-nighters. There are increasing numbers of kids who are in terrible fear of failure and will look to whatever means to cope with the pressures.

Energetic parental involvement reduces the likelihood that your teenager will participate in high-risk behavior, including drugs and binge drinking. In fact, parental judgment weighs heavily in how our kids view drugs and drinking. Common sense dictates that we communicate with our children and guide them in the right direction. Kids who know that their parents disapprove of substance abuse are significantly less likely to abuse alcohol or drugs. However, parental disapproval is no longer the consensus, as the above case with Nigella Lawson illustrates.

As a country we are moving in the direction of legalizing substances that negatively affect our kids, mentally and physically. There is a strong correlation between pot use and the loss of IQ points. Research underscores the fact that soft drugs are frequently a gateway to harder drugs. Science tells us that hard drugs kill thousands of human beings every year. Fortunately, research also tells us this: energetic parental involvement significantly reduces the chances that a child will abuse drugs.[3]

First we must ask ourselves about our own use of drugs and alcohol. Prozac and the like do control anxiety and panic, but medicine does not deal with root causes. It blunts the edge of the depression. Therefore it may also serve to depress the desire of a dependent mom to get real help and receive true inner healing. This is what happened to my mom. She felt better when she used drugs, but they blunted her desire to enter counseling. The etymology of the word *narcotics* is revealing: it is from a Greek word meaning "to get numb." Numbing ourselves is unhelpful in facing reality. It certainly won't give us the power to overcome our challenges. It will in fact numb our ability to turn to the one power that will help, and that is the power of the Holy Spirit. We must be honest with ourselves about our own behavior before we can look to our children's behavior.

God does not want moms to be depressed and longing to numb that depression. I sadly know a number of moms, Christian moms, in this situation. They drink alcohol at night, hiding what they do from their families. They are on all sorts of painkillers, hoping to get through another depressed day. I had one friend from a Christian family who is now in an institution because not only she but also her husband tried to hide from the deep problems. Being a Christian does not mean we should be ashamed to admit we need help from friends or professionals. In fact, the life of faith is the life of truth. On our down days, and every mom has them, we have to develop alternatives to drinking one more glass of wine. The best alternative is to live in God's love. Life is not a tightrope where one wrong move will kill us. We are surrounded by God's goodness; He is not disappointed with us and we should not be wallowing in regret and defeat no matter our circumstances. I believe this more than ever even though I am struggling physically more than I have before.

In terms of our children, any intemperate drug use on our part will hinder our example to our children. Get help and show your kids that you are getting help. We cannot pretend to our kids. After all, they love us, and they look to us searchingly. We must be humble and apologize when we fail—and then get help. This will also serve as a wonderful example to your family. We all fail, but it is what we do with that failure that can give God the glory. It can also give our children the ability to embrace failure and turn it into something good.

Almost all communities in America are affected by drug use and other self-destructive behaviors. If adult consensus exists in a community that teens need to be held accountable, then appropriate action is usually taken. This is a great comfort to parents. However, if the community has resigned itself to defeat, then usually what happens is a culture of silence in the face of a challenging issue. But as someone once said, "All it takes for evil to triumph is for good men to do nothing." Silence and resigned acceptance to something we know is wrong are never the appropriate responses of a wise parent. Those almost always lead to even larger failures.

My son Daniel regularly witnessed drug transactions in the hallways and bathrooms of his high school in New Hampshire. There was a police car parked at the school every day. The extent of the drug problem was hitting the local newspapers, and there were drug arrests among the students. My husband and I tried to prod various officials at school into action. The town next to Hanover had voted to bring police into the building to patrol the hallways to stop the drug dealing. One day, Daniel accompanied us to see his guidance counselor about the college application process. At the end of the conversation, we brought up the drug problem, saying that we had called school leadership including the principal, but no one was doing anything about it. The guidance counselor denied knowing anything. Daniel had disbelief on his face.

Today we cannot assume that the responsible adults in our children's lives are making the right judgment calls, because doing so requires both courage and action. Our response to collective silence cannot mirror the status quo. We must aggressively advocate for our children and drug-free schools, no matter how much of an uphill battle it might be. Even more importantly, we must be sure that we are setting a good example for our children. We must let them know in no uncertain terms that while it may be fine in our family for an adult to enjoy a glass of wine, we completely oppose overindulging under any circumstances because it is clear in the book of Proverbs that getting drunk destroys wisdom:

> Wine is a mocker and beer a brawler;
> whoever is led astray by them is not wise. (20:1)

In this day and age, kids have access to drugs that they don't even have to buy. Some just rifle through their parents' medicine cabinets getting all the drugs they want. On a lovely, sunny day in Palo Alto, I got into a serious discussion with another mom named Karen about the proliferation of drugs in our town and the terrible effect it was having in our schools.

Karen felt compelled to unburden herself. One of her children was in constant trouble with the police and school; he was currently in rehab. The last time he was picked up by the police, Karen and her husband told the policeman to arrest the boy. He had a whole stash of prescription drugs he had been given by a classmate. Karen and her husband hoped that the shock of facing legal consequences might galvanize their sixteen-year-old to wake up to the fact that he was in danger of destroying his life.

The police refused to arrest the boy because too many affluent Palo Alto parents have made legal action into an art form. The police want the parents to be in charge, naturally enough. The drugs had come from another boy's parents' medicine cabinet. Karen called the boy's family to complain about the ready accessibility of the meds. The other mom could only plead, "Don't call our boys drug addicts because that will make them so." Karen and her husband eventually sent their son to rehab. She ended by saying, "Well, I guess our kids need to learn how to blossom where they're planted."

My friends, it is quite clear that many in our children's generation are not blooming where they are planted. That is why moves can be an effective parental tool. My daughter was offered drugs by another fifth grader. We put her in a private school because the principal of the first school was turning a blind eye to what was occurring under her very nose. At school some battles are absolutely worth fighting. Ultimately a mom's goal has to be to protect her child from unsafe situations. Drastic action may be called for. Sometimes it is the only wise course.

ROCK AND ROLL

Rock and roll epitomizes a culture that encompasses not only music but also a lifestyle in the pursuit of fame. Kids hear the most outrageous things through certain kinds of secular music. It is clear that our kids are adversely affected by the raunchy, sexualized language and by the complete disrespect for authority that permeates much of what I will call the rock and roll culture. Making one's home a haven where inappropriate music, language, behavior, and movies are not allowed helps build standards for our kids.

As a society we are all over the place in terms of what is allowed and what is not. My six-year-old son was invited to watch the movie *Titanic* during a play date. Sex scenes at the age of six are wildly inappropriate, and in fact the Bible is clear that we should "set no wicked thing before mine eyes" (Ps. 101:3 KJV). How much more should we protect our kids of tender age? Moms are called to use their discernment every day, so don't be afraid to make tough calls. Do not get sidetracked by this kind of argumentation.

We moms have to understand what our kids are watching, what they are listening to, and the social media they are using. Participate with your kids and preview movies, books, and websites. Establish guidelines of what is appropriate. Discuss music, books, and movies with your kids. Keep introducing your kids to beauty and faith through great music, art, and culture. Do not allow music, electronics, and social media to become babysitters for your kids. This is a temptation that I myself have fallen into, especially now that my health is frail. But we have to make sure that our kids are not filling their time with images and sounds that will tear them down. Idle hands are the devil's workshop. It is imperative that we create an environment for and with our children that is conducive to right living.

We have to deal with the entertainment culture in the daily lives of our children. Our kids cannot be allowed to make web entertainment an idol. In my home, our boys struggle to turn off the electronics, especially computer games and video games. Our daughter gets caught up in social media. We cannot allow these distractions to take over their—and our—world. We must be daily vigilant to draw the attention of this generation back into the world of the living. Exercise deep control of this aspect in your own life. Since few of us have a family farm that requires kids to roll up their sleeves and get into heavy-duty chores after school, our kids can get swept up in entertaining themselves. Sports and extracurricular activities are crucial, as is a daily routine of chores.

In our family, having a child ten years younger has effectively brought real-life chores to the elder kids. We were very fortunate with the surprise birth of Nicky. I had built-in babysitters from the start. This created useful roles for the older kids, and I quickly came to appreciate the value of many hands lightening my workload. I also appreciated the fact that the older kids are so invested in our youngest. They have played a vital role in raising Nicky, and that has been a blessing.

Kids like feeling useful. Finding good tasks for the kids is something I pray about. The Lord is not offended when we draw Him into our daily lives; in fact, He loves being asked about the details. One of my favorite scriptures is Psalm 139:17:

> How precious also are Your thoughts to me, O God!
> How great is the sum of them! (NKJV)

God thinks about us all the time! When I came across this verse years ago, I was blown away. I think about the Lord all the time, but that is nothing in comparison to how much He thinks about all His children. He wants to be intimately involved in our daily activities. These activities will serve as an important buffer to worldly temptations.

FAME

There exists today an outsized desire to be famous. Many people are seeking their "fifteen minutes of fame." The rock-and-roll culture fans the false hopes of fame. Even my own kids have been affected by it. I was driving with the kids one fine day when our twelve-year-old daughter suddenly announced, "I want to be famous one day, but I am unsure what will make me famous." Her words have lingered long in my memory. Celebrity, and the desire for it, is permeating every aspect of media today. I think this is fueled by a number of factors, but within everyone exists a desire to be known, to be respected, and to be loved. Our kids have to know that at home they have exactly that—they are known, respected, and loved.

Children don't want to be invisible to those closest to them. Being part of a loving family and having connections to church and community brings a sense of personal value that cannot be underestimated. Feeling invisible and uncherished is one of the reasons social media is becoming an increasing presence in the lives of our children. *People* magazine may not write a profile on an anonymous teenager's life, but she can put it all out there on the web. Fame on the Internet is not a healthy goal for any child. Please be vigilant about your child's Internet life, and if you have to confiscate cell phones and shut down computers, so be it. There also are many parental programs available so you can monitor your children's e-mails and computer use if you discern a problem with your child's growing use, or overuse, of social media.

THE OCCULT

On the issue of the occult, let me quote the famous Russian general's orders at the Battle of Stalingrad: "Not one step back." There has to be zero tolerance toward the demonic. Girls especially are being lured into the supernatural through the preponderance of juvenile literature on the occult. I recently wandered into the teen section of our hometown library and the number of books on the supernatural, almost to the exclusion of all else, was astounding. This teenage section was dominated by stories of witches and warlocks. Due to the success of the Harry Potter series, the publishing industry pushes this stuff on our kids because it sells. Librarians, teachers, and parents, desperate to get kids to read anything, go along for the ride. My own experience as a homeschooling mom proves that children respond to really good writing as much as they are attracted by a particular subject. Great writing awakens the mind of youngsters; it does not intimidate them. We do not have to choose ghastly subjects just to get our kids reading.

On another level, this fascination with the occult comes from a very dark place. Educate yourself on this issue, and have open discussions with your kids on this subject. The occult flourishes in parental ignorance. Don't underestimate its powers just because you don't understand it. The chief spokesman for the occult, Aleister Crowley, was a twentieth-century Englishman who wrote the definitive book on satanism. It is widely believed that Crowley said the greatest commandment for satanists is, "Do what thou wilt shall be the whole of the law." Satanists glorify the self and make doing what is right in our own eyes the ultimate good. Sound familiar? Our culture increasingly reflects this desire to feed the self without regard to anything or anyone else. We just have to look back to the famous passage in Isaiah 14 about Lucifer to see that the "I will's" are at the heart of rebellion toward God:

You said in your heart,
I will ascend to the heavens;
I will raise my throne above the stars of God. (v. 13)

Take control of what your children are reading and watching. My youngest son says that approximately 80 percent of the books read by his peers are focused on fantasy, demons, and the supernatural. And don't give up when your child is older. Your children will need even more help in cultivating a countercultural taste in literature as they become teens. As parents, we need to be aware if our children are reading books on the supernatural, using Ouija boards, having séances, or putting hexes on others—even if it is all done seemingly in fun. Putting a stop to it right away is critical. Better yet, don't let it occur in the first place. The occult is a dark area where real, negative power does exist.

We have dear friends whose daughter played around with the occult. Her dad is a pastor and her mom is a lovely Christian woman. The daughter is now institutionalized. While there were other factors in this sad story, including the use of drugs, there is no doubt that her playing around with the occult was followed quickly by mental instability and then mental breakdown. This should not surprise any believer. Jesus spoke very clearly about the devil. First Peter 5:8 tells us that the devil "prowls around like a roaring lion looking for someone to devour." It is no surprise that he wants to devour our children.

We cannot take for granted the spiritual safety of our families. We have to be a hedge of spiritual protection around our kids because once these influences come into their lives, it is hard to dislodge them. Look to your pastor or priest for guidance and spiritual help. The good news in this? We do not live in a Star Wars universe where the forces of good battle equal forces of evil; we live in a world where good has triumphed in Jesus. Remember Psalm 62:11:

> One thing God has spoken,
> two things I have heard:
> "Power belongs to you, God."

Raising Teenagers

Now that several of our kids are in their twenties, I see that it was even more important for me to be at home with them as teenagers than when they were very young. My father always said "small kids, small problems—big kids, big problems." However, if we have laid the foundation of love, faith, virtue, and prayer in our homes from an early age, we will reap in their teen years. My relationship with our kids has gotten deeper and richer with time. I do not take this for granted. We have, of course, experienced the consequences of poor choices by our teenagers. But we remain committed to their maturity and growth over time as they learn from their mistakes. As a mom, I have found power from what I call the three Cs (communication, community, and collective wisdom) in bolstering my ability to help our kids through turbulent times.

In a time of material plenty, we live in a culture that

increasingly offers empty promises of happiness if we simply live for ourselves and not worry about right and wrong. By providing our children, especially our teens, with a strong inner core that comes from a clear sense of right and wrong, we can counteract the prevailing morality of "do whatever feels good." God has given us a set of ethics to live by in the Ten Commandments. For thousands of years, the Ten Commandments have been the foundation of moral truth for Western civilization, helping distinguish between good and evil, true and false, right and wrong. If we depart from this path, or if we fail to teach it to our children, we do so at great peril. Our children learn wisdom through being taught right from wrong. As Christian parents we respect and revere God. We know that "the fear of the LORD is the beginning of wisdom" (Ps. 111:10). If we fear and respect His commands, we will have the basis for making wise decisions.

Ponder

God's Word

Rejoice always, pray continually, give thanks in all
circumstances. (1 Thess. 5:16–18)
One thing God has spoken,
two things I have heard:
"Power belongs to you, God." (Ps. 62:11)
How precious also are Your thoughts to me, O God!
How great is the sum of them! (Ps. 139:17 NKJV)

The Authors' Words

"No matter what the world is saying about our faith,
our kids have to be confident that Christianity is worthy
of their lives."

Assess

1. Are you raising children who know their history—
   specifically the incredible good that Christians have
   been responsible for in our world?
2. In which of the following areas are you afraid to reason
   with or challenge your child: the devaluing nature of
   casual sex, the need to stay free from drugs, the trap of
   electronics, or the lure of the occult?
3. What areas in your own life need a touch from God so
   that you can model a godly marriage full of intimacy

and respect, a life filled with the Holy Spirit, and a simple lifestyle focused on God and others?

4. Are you able to speak fully and freely with your spouse about concerns you have for your children? Why or why not? If not, how might you change that negative pattern?

5. Where does your family most need God's help? Are you and your husband consistently seeking His help in that area? Why or why not?

Sum Up

We are not called to be our kids' friends; they will have plenty of those in life. We are called to be their parents who use discernment in the raising of their kids. If we do our job wisely, we will develop a bond with them that will never be broken, no matter the circumstance.

Eight

Encouragement: It's a Discipline

E ncouragement and discipline are inextricably intertwined; one cannot exist without the other in the raising of our children. We cannot discipline our children without cheering them on because they will become fearful of our judgment and most likely become very judgmental themselves. Continuous praise to the detriment of truth and consequences will result in kids who will remain kids with no understanding of wisdom. In my experience, disciplining my kids has meant that I myself must be very disciplined. If I don't put in the energy and emotion required to encourage and discipline my kids, it does not happen by magic. The following two stories, both true, illustrate my point.

THE STORY OF ELI AND HIS SONS

Eli was a famous minister in the temple of Israel during the Old Testament period (1 Sam. 2:12–36). He served the Lord and

His people on many different occasions. He was a good man. Unfortunately, he did not properly encourage his sons to do good or discipline them when they did evil. Perhaps he was just "too busy" to take the time to discipline his kids.

God warned Eli about his lack of proper parenting numerous times. God cares deeply that we are parents who encourage and discipline our children. But Eli chose to do nothing, and in my experience as a mom doing nothing almost never works. As adults, Eli's sons took advantage of their position as sons of the powerful high priest of Israel. They robbed the temple, extorted money from the people, and lived immoral lives. Yet Eli's attention was elsewhere, and he continued to let their behavior slide. His sons went from bad to worse and all Israel knew; the truth does surface even if we try our best to ignore it. In the end, the Lord caused all of Eli's sons to perish on the same day Eli himself died. His line was completely obliterated from the face of the earth. This dramatic episode bears witness to God's desire for us to raise virtuous children. If Eli had done his duty to properly encourage and effectively discipline his children, their end would surely have been quite different.

In my own life I have been deeply encouraged by my friend Linda. Linda symbolizes what good parenting can do even in very difficult situations. Linda is a kind lady who deeply loves her family. Linda married her college sweetheart, Tom. They were married for over twenty years, and in the early years of their marriage they were united in their desire to raise their kids well and in faith. The last few years of their marriage were rocky, but nothing prepared her for her husband's sudden announcement that he was unhappy and he wanted a divorce. Tom left her for a younger woman with whom he had been having an affair.

Linda did not give up raising her teenage kids to respect her husband even though during the divorce proceedings he did terrible things to her; when people feel guilty they often do horrible things to bring the innocent down with them. He even had excrement thrown on her car during the proceedings. This ugly incident was symbolic of the vitriol that was being directed at Linda from the very beginning of the separation. Linda worked hard for her two kids not to be caught in the middle. Her daughter was thoroughly bewildered and started to live a wild life. Linda, however, did not give up praying and seeking to set an example by taking the higher road of forgiveness. It took several years, but ultimately Linda's ministry to her children has borne very good fruit. The early years of disciplining her daughter, combined with Linda's continued godly example, became the foundation of reconciliation. Ultimately, we do reap what we sow if we do not grow weary.

Discipline, along with encouragement, is a vital component of our ministry to our children. Discipline means bringing up our kids with a sense of honor and virtue, which will allow our kids to grow in character, maturity, and confidence over time. Gregory and I try to give our kids ten parts encouragement and love for every one part discipline. Both elements are essential counterparts if we do not want to raise kids who feel judged by their parents and found wanting. Gregory and I give our children warm expressions of love and encouragement because this allows us to exercise tough discipline when needed. First and foremost, our children know that they are loved and accepted, no matter their behavior. However, certain actions on their part are not acceptable in our family and through our bonds of love, we have established our loving authority over them.

Disciplining our kids will allow us to bypass this current

obsession with adolescent behavior for adults who should know better. Our society sadly allows its youth to stretch adolescence into their thirties and beyond. We have many adults who are still groping for their identity as if they were still teenagers, with their families picking up the pieces. Recently, I caught a commercial advertising a dating service for the fifty-and-over crowd and one woman cooed, "I feel as if I am back in high school"—as if that were a good thing.

The word *virtue* shares the same Latin root as the word *courage*. Virtue is courage in the face of temptation. Virtue is informed by the wisdom learned from parents, mentors, quality friends, and through the study of the Scriptures. Virtue does not materialize out of thin air. I know that I have mentioned the energy required in the disciplining of our children, but let me mention it again. This is where I fall down—it is all too easy to give up and give in, but it is clear that energy and consistency are required while disciplining our children; there are simply no known substitutes. Discipline should never be done in anger but in the understanding that our children must learn that their actions have consequences. As the Bible teaches, all of us will eventually reap exactly what we sow (Gal. 6:7).

The Lord has given us parental authority as a ministry to our children. We have to accept this ministry; otherwise, our children will raise themselves according to the world's standards. Discipline is for our children's edification and growth. Our children are to be raised to respect us and to respect our authority. This reflects the respect we are to give to our eternal Father and His authority over us.

It is no mistake that the word *fear* is used at least three hundred times in the Bible in relation to God. This is because our heavenly Father is awe-inspiring. This is a fear based on respect and reverence. For the believer, this fear brings many benefits. Wisdom, so necessary for a mom, flows from a right attitude before God: "the fear of the LORD is the beginning of wisdom" (Prov. 9:10). The reverence of God instructs our parenting.

EXERCISING OUR PARENTAL AUTHORITY

Today, it is beyond unfortunate that so many parents have abdicated their God-given parental authority. Far too many kids are being left to raise themselves, often with disastrous results. Our discipline is one important way that our children understand their actions have consequences that they must bear. Encouragement helps them take on the responsibilities that will help them grow into mature and trustworthy adults.

Becoming parents comes with the responsibility to raise children with instruction and guidance. That is what discipline is: instruction and guidance. If we are to discipline our children wisely, we, too, require His discipline, His instruction, and His guidance. The Holy Spirit is our guide and tutor. He will direct our path, He will teach us the way in which to go with our kids, and He will give us the energy we need if we humbly ask. But we must also obey what He has shown us to do. For just like a good teacher, the Holy Spirit will not progress onto the next lesson until we have mastered the one He is trying to teach us.

Proverbs 13:13 tells us,

> Whoever scorns instruction will pay for it,
> but whoever respects a command is rewarded.

As moms we must know that parental encouragement and discipline will yield peace in our children. Consequences should never be meted out in order to wreak vengeance; quite the opposite. Our children must understand that life brings the responsibility to act respectfully and in accordance with God's laws. We must remember that even though children can be so cute and cuddly, "Foolishness is bound up in the heart of a child" (Prov. 22:15 NKJV). It is only through consistent love, encouragement, and discipline that our children will grow to be respectful, responsible adults who will experience fullness and not brokenness in their lives.

WISDOM IS KEY IN DISCIPLINE AND ENCOURAGEMENT

Wisdom is key in disciplining and encouraging our children effectively. The Bible teaches us about a great mother:

> She opens her mouth with wisdom,
> and on her tongue is the law of kindness.
> (Prov. 31:26 NKJV)

Wisdom is from the Greek word *sophos*, and it means "being able to judge what is true and right." Wisdom gives us discernment, which is the ability to understand reality in different situations and thereby make good decisions. Wise living begets a good life. Discernment will help us, and eventually our kids, to make good choices.

God disciplines those whom He loves. This truth is referenced both in the Old Testament and the New Testament. Hebrews 12:6 tells us,

The Lord disciplines the one he loves,
and he chastens everyone he accepts as his son.

It is for our good that we experience His reproof in our lives. Sadly, I have come to see that I am more stubborn as an adult than I was as a child. Therefore the chastening is longer and more painful. But I realize that it is done for my benefit so that I might reap the healing that comes from repentance and the peace that flows from right living.

Choosing not to discipline is a grave injustice to your children. You may be sick, you may be tired, you feel yourself to be too busy, but you cannot leave your children to raise themselves. This is a crucial point in parenting. As adults your children will face the consequences of their actions. Their childhood is our opportunity to teach them the blessings of good choices anchored in wisdom or the difficult fruit of poor choices. Doing so when they are young and malleable is so much more effective, and humane, than leaving them to learn these truths on their own later in their lives.

Gregory and I have been the recipients of unpleasant calls informing us of bad behavior on the part of our kids. Most parents have to go through this. Gregory and I pray for this kind of reality check. We have allowed consequences to flow, even when we were in a position to stop them. This has been painful in the short run, but all to the good for our children over time.

In the long run our children are the losers when we become the buffer between bad behavior and its logical consequences. We have to let reality come in even when the timing is inconvenient or the truth is difficult. We have to forego easy shortcuts in our own lives and in the lives of our children. We must consistently encourage and discipline our children over the years, for from this sowing they will reap a harvest of mature wisdom.

One reason for not disciplining is that we are so busy we hope for the best, whatever that means. We feel we do not have the required energy, or time, to deal with our kids' difficult situation. We want to help them; we know that we are called to do so, but we just don't know how to fit it into our schedules. I am busy, and my husband is busy, but the kids have come first in the limited time we have with them. This does not mean that they are the center of the universe, even our universe, or that our lives are complete if only they are happy and successful. It means that there is no substitute for the time we spend encouraging and disciplining them year in and year out. Investing time today in age-appropriate discipline can save months of dealing with disciplinary action from your children's university or worse, the police and the court system in ten or fifteen years. It is an investment you're making today in your children's future and your own.

Some parents do not discipline appropriately because they themselves are deeply broken. They cannot accept discipline for themselves, let alone for their kids. This area has to be addressed by the Holy Spirit. If you see another family in this situation, deep intercessory prayer is called for. If you feel you yourself or your spouse might be in this situation, please speak with your pastor or priest at length. Please get qualified professional help so that you can make progress. The future of your family depends on it. We know that God's arm is never too short to save (Isa. 59:1), but these situations are complex. From my own experience with brokenness, it is only the work of the Holy Spirit over time that brings true healing. But we must do our part: repenting, forgiving, and seeking guidance and healing.

It is a long road back to wholeness, but the Holy Spirit can lead the way.

REPENTANCE

Repentance is a key part of the healing process, both for ourselves and our kids. Our children must understand the importance of repentance. Not only can repentance begin to repair damaged relationships, it can help children begin the often long and hard process of turning away from the behavior that caused them to make poor choices. If our children understand the many deep benefits that come through repentance, they will be less stubborn when called to repent. And if moms make repentance a normal part of reconciliation, kids will not shy away from it.

Moms have to direct children to repentance and reformation. We cannot allow our kids to blame others for their poor choices. This is a very common strategy and is as old as time. It began with Adam in the Garden of Eden blaming Eve for eating the forbidden fruit. Eve of course blamed the serpent . . . and so it goes today. This is not the path our children should be allowed to take if parents want to truly resolve sin. It is clear that God views each person as responsible for his or her own actions. The Holy Spirit will give the strength to repent and the strength to begin the path to turn away from sin and bad habits.

ACCOUNTABILITY INSTEAD OF BLAME SHIFTING

Being accountable for our behavior is part of the process of healing. God is forgiving, and He is compassionate. He knows our situation better than we do. Recognition of sin, taking owner-ship of one's behavior, and not shifting guilt and blame onto someone else means that repentance is required. If we are not humble enough to confess our sins, we will not move forward in our lives. This will stunt the process of healing and wholeness that our heavenly Father wants to bring to us all.

We want to be the parents from whom our children seek wisdom. The virtuous woman spoken of in Proverbs 31:10–31 is a woman who speaks wisdom and faithful instruction, and her children will rise up and call her blessed. I am convinced our children want the truth from us, even when it is painful. Our children want the security that honesty and truth bring, even when it is difficult truth.

While we do not want our children to be afraid of us, we want them to have a reverence for God. Reverence for God and His ways is a sure path to wisdom. Ultimately each child must be brought into the kingdom of God through his or her own relationship with the Lord. But we as parents must show the same reverence for God that we expect our kids to have for Him, for "do as I say, but not as I do" is a parenting disaster.

ALLOWING OUR CHILDREN TO FACE CONSEQUENCES

Kids do not always understand why they are making poor choices. They at times do not feel like walking in the truth, but when they come to you with their poor choices, they are not coming for phony validation. In their heart of hearts, they want you to love them enough to stand up for the truth and to be there for them when they have to face the consequences. They really want to hear the following: they are loved, they are forgiven, and there is redemption for them and their situation.

Proverbs 29:15 tells us,

> A rod and a reprimand impart wisdom,
> but a child left undisciplined disgraces its mother.

I believe there are different routes to effective discipline. I know many good parents who use controlled physical punishment like a light spanking for young children when they have failed to obey other, gentler methods of correction. They feel comfortable with this form of discipline, and they argue persuasively that spanking is healthier than descending into verbal abuse. We know other equally great moms and dads who would never think of using corporal punishment of any kind. I have come to the conclusion that discipline, like so much in mothering, is governed by discernment, your child's personality, and your personal convictions.

If you are opposed to spanking, do not persuade yourself that it is a good thing for you and your spouse to use corporal punishment. If, however, you believe that a quick, controlled spanking (appropriate only to a certain age and after other gentler disciplines have been ignored) will serve your child, then feel at peace. Certainly the Bible does support such action if done in love and always with the child's best interests in mind. Love and consistency are key.

Also note that we ourselves need to be in order for our kids to be in order. The Bible does not lay out a laundry list of dos and don'ts for moms because a woman who is living a functional, healthy life with a strong spiritual connection has mothering under control; a woman whose life is out of control will not be able to compartmentalize her mothering and protect her children from her poor choices. And since much more is caught than is taught, it is likely that her children will follow in the footsteps of her poor choices.

THE POWER OF WORDS AND CRITICISM

There is one form of discipline that, while pervasive, is never justifiable. That is disciplining through constant negative criticism. I was raised by parents who criticized me as a form of discipline. Trust me, it does not work. Raising children does require frequent pruning, but it requires even more nurturing. Remember the 10 to 1 rule: ten parts love and affirmation for every one part discipline. Contempt and disdain have no place in mothering. If your children only hear an unending litany of complaints and criticisms, they will come to question not only your judgment (a defensive move in order not to feel bad about themselves), but they will be forced to question something even more precious: your love for them.

Words are either poison or fruit: wise mothers understand the power of words. As it is written in Proverbs 18:21: "The tongue has the power of life and death." Words kill, and words give life. Contempt and disdain, as well as toxic gossip, have no place in mothering. Refrain from bringing up old failings because a regurgitation of the past actually reflects an unforgiving spirit. Our kids are first broken by our criticisms; then they build barriers. These barriers are very difficult to overcome in the future. As adults, your children will avoid spending time with you if this was their experience when they were young.

There is a very powerful verse for moms in the Bible about anger: "Be angry, and do not sin" (Eph. 4:26 NKJV). Moms do become angry, often with justification. In my own personal life, I don't get angry at the drop of a hat. But when I am pressed by a child's nonresponse, I can and do proceed with vigor. However, there are times I cross the line (because I do scream), and I have to be humble and apologize. But I love the verse, "Come now, and let us reason together" (Isa. 1:18 NKJV), and the fact that we can, and should, bring reason to our discussion with our kids. They have to be brought into a dialogue because motherhood is not a monologue.

Family conversations are a dynamic dialogue with multiple parties: our spouse, our children, and the Lord. Kids want to have discussions. Learn to use this effectively in your discipline of your children. Discussions become critical as they grow older. Even small children need to be in deep discussions that are age-appropriate. This helps them wrestle with key issues and grow in their reasoning and communication skills. Sometimes these discussions start with an apology from our side.

BE A LIFE GIVER

If we need to apologize to our children, we must be humble and do so. My parents were old-school. They believed it would be demeaning to apologize to my brother and me. I have not found this to be true at all. My husband and I know when we cross the line. We know that by *not* apologizing we will lose the respect, not to mention the love, of our children in the long run. This is especially true of adult children. Respect is built on trust and years of our being responsible and committed, not on our being perfect. Our being able to apologize and repent when necessary sets a good example for the kids. When kids do the wrong thing but seek our forgiveness sincerely, we have to be quick to forgive and make sure that, to the best of their ability, they have cleaned up whatever mess they have made.

Allow the Holy Spirit to bring the power of forgiveness into your heart, and do not allow yourself to go to bed angry with your kids. Forgiveness will bring freedom and the ability for our family to release bitterness, resentment, and disappointment. Forgiveness will be the backbone of our encouragement and discipline of our children. We as parents want to encourage out of a heart of love, not out of a heart of bitterness and anger.

Children are vulnerable, even if teenagers don't always look it. A verbal assault may cause hurt that can reverberate through the years. Do not kill your child's soul with constant criticism because criticism destroys relationships. Don't give into your feelings of frustration by belittling your child. If your own parents had difficulty in choosing their words, if they made you feel small, you may very well be handicapped in verbalizing life-giving words to your children. Be honest with your spouse and mentors and seek help. Learn to communicate constructively. Words of encouragement, laughter, and love bring life. Words of criticism and condemnation bring death. Be a life giver to your children.

Ponder

God's Word

Whoever scorns instruction will pay for it,
but whoever respects a command is rewarded. (Prov. 13:13)
My son, do not make light of the Lord's discipline,
and do not lose heart when he rebukes you,
because the Lord disciplines the one he loves,
and he chastens everyone he accepts as his son.
   (Heb. 12:5–6)

Everything that was written in the past was written to teach us, so that through the endurance taught in the Scriptures and the encouragement they provide we might have hope. (Rom. 15:4)

The Authors' Words

"Remember the 10 to 1 rule: ten parts love and affirmation for every one part discipline. Contempt and disdain have no place in mothering."

Assess

1. What keeps you from disciplining your children?
   · Too cute? (*In the early ages, sometimes disobedience looks adorable!*)
   · Too affluent? (*My money can get them out of trouble.*)
   · Too busy? (*Everything else I am doing is more urgent.*)

- Too tired? (*I am only human after all!*)
- Too hurt from harsh treatment in your own past? (*I don't want my kids to hate me like I hate my parents.*)

2. Recall a time in your own life when you were deeply grateful for a word of rebuke or warning or discipline.
3. Recall a time in your own life when you were motivated to excellence or integrity by a word of encouragement.
4. How are you (and your spouse) doing with the 10 to 1 rule (ten parts love and encouragement for every one part discipline and correction)? Where would you say you are on that scale? Is there room for improvement?
5. Are you allowing your children to reap the consequences of their actions (both good and bad) in an age-appropriate way? Or are you sheltering your kids from reality too much? If so, why?

Sum Up

Discipline is essential because it helps our children understand that their actions have consequences they must bear whether for good or ill. We use encouragement to help our children take on the responsibilities that will help them grow into mature and trustworthy adults. Ten parts encouragement and one part discipline is essential for our kids' development.

Nine

The Three Cs of Motherhood: Communication, Collective Wisdom, and Community

Loneliness is a growing problem in the United States. This is having an impact on moms. I believe that the increasing desire for celebrity stems in part from this feeling of isolation and feeling invisible in our society. Individuals feel invisible because they feel uncared for. Chicago psychology professor John T. Cacioppo coauthored a book entitled *Loneliness: Human Nature and the Need for Social Connection*. Through extensive research he and his coauthor estimate that close to sixty million Americans suffer from loneliness.[1] Moms who are from broken families, or who relocate for various reasons, can feel disconnected.

In Palo Alto I went to the playground every day with our

children; every day it was just the nannies and me. The fact that many of us work outside the home contributes to the fact that we don't necessarily have the channels of support from other moms that were so readily available in prior generations. Without communication, without community, we are left with the feeling of being unanchored to communal wisdom and isolated in our decision-making process. These are very serious issues for moms as we are all in real need of wise advice, encouragement, and counsel.

Isolation, for us as moms and for our children, is a growing problem that we must counteract with determination. Because we as a family have moved many times, I can tell you that it is not through wishing that community is formed. It is through hard work, with hospitality being a key ingredient.

COMMUNICATION: TWO EARS AND ONE MOUTH

In Deuteronomy 6:6–7 God stresses the importance of communicating with our children: "These commandments that I give you today are to be on your hearts. Impress them on your children. Talk about them when you sit at home and when you walk along the road, when you lie down and when you get up." Communication is crucial, as any counselor will tell you; there can be no excuses when we choose to stop communicating with our family members. Women are blessed because most of us love to communicate and build relationships. However, it is as crucial to listen as it is to speak in communication, and this is especially true with our growing kids.

As babies, in order to learn to speak we must first learn to listen. This is true of our relationship with the Lord: "Be still, and know that I am God" (Ps. 46:10). The quality of our listening determines in large part the strength of our relationships with our spouse and our friends. It is also a powerful ingredient in our developing relationship with our growing children. Listening to your children is key to having a good relationship with them. Through our listening, over time our kids will reveal who they are deep down. Listening will take into account how they are evolving and who they are becoming as they grow up and become independent.

As parents, we need to build relationships filled with communication and trust. We want our children, even when they are adults, to turn to us for counsel. They will not do so if they feel rejected or if they feel we are not trustworthy or really don't care that much. Our children need to know that when they confess their failings to us we are listening first, and we will then act according to our great love and respect for them.

It is up to you as the parent to make sure that your children are not afraid of you and your judgment. Respecting your parental authority is vital, but if that respect turns into fear then you will have serious problems communicating with your children. You absolutely want to be the one they turn to in any circumstance. Our kids have communicated very difficult things to Gregory and me. It is hard not to beat ourselves up at times for how we have failed as parents. We have to be respectful of our children's privacy, but trust me, we know our kids have made choices they regret and we regret. But I bear witness that open communication has allowed our relationship to weather some very bad storms. Communication, trust, and love have been key. We have also not hesitated to allow discipline and consequences to take their course.

Teenage kids are notoriously fickle in their communication, but I have found several simple, albeit time-consuming, avenues of communication available to all parents. Hanging out in the kitchen together is one way to promote important conversations with your kids. Even if you hate to cook, learn how to make chocolate chip cookies and some simple, homemade meals. Unlike our grandmothers, our generation does not seem to cook much. But giving up the kitchen as a center of communication is unwise. Kids always find their way to the kitchen, so use it to your advantage. Always eating on the run eliminates one of the most important avenues for communication we have today as families. Making time to sit down and enjoy even a very simple meal together is a blessing for one and all.

Love as evidenced by hospitality and food at the dinner table takes on spiritual overtones. Create a convivial atmosphere around the kitchen table for your family no matter how busy the family is. Even if you buy takeout, don't stand at the kitchen island but sit down and have a good conversation. Treat your children as you would civilized adults, and they will grow up to be civilized adults. More importantly, they will look forward to mealtimes where they get to spend time together. Too often in this busy world we eat in our cars or pell-mell in the kitchen. Sitting down to eat meals will require effort, but if we give up eating together, we will be giving up one of our most effective communication venues.

HOSPITALITY: BUILD RELATIONSHIPS THROUGH KINDNESS

The Bible itself encourages us to entertain others and to do it generously. We want our homes to be warm and welcoming, and we want people to enjoy our homes and hospitality. This is an art, one that we are in danger of losing in the current climate of busy. My mom was my great example in hospitality, and I am thankful for her good example. But I have friends who come from families where hospitality was fraught with tension because it represented work, and in the eyes of some women, judgment. Moms (including myself) can run around shouting to the troops (husband and children): Is the bathroom clean? Have you dusted and vacuumed? Are you dressed yet? Is the table set? No wonder more and more people are retreating to restaurants to do their entertaining.

A friend called me once after a fun dinner party I had hosted and asked for help in developing her own hostess skills. She loved her mom and had a good relationship with her, but every time guests came over, the family had to deal with "Mom changing into Mr. Hyde" because she was anxious about every detail. As a result, having guests over was something my friend never wanted to do. I spent time with her, which I really enjoyed, and I think the mentoring helped her develop something important in her life. Look for mentors if being hospitable does not come naturally. We were not created to go it alone, and some of us must unbend enough to ask for help.

If we are hospitable, our children will find it much easier to be hospitable. Hospitality builds community. Your kids will thank you for it, and they in turn will have the gift of hospitality when they are adults. Through the years, I have kept my children's Mother's Day cards, and invariably each child at some point would write about my being a chef, or in the words of five-year-old Christian, a "good cooker." But the truth is: I don't love cooking. What I love is the time it gives me to interact with my family over a meal. I can usually get one or more of our children involved in a good discussion while we prepare the food together. The communication that occurs while cooking makes it all worthwhile.

CONVERSATIONS

Like many moms, for years I have shuttled kids to every activity known to man. It is enlightening how much one learns in the car with a gaggle of kids in the back. It can be tedious and time-consuming to drive to an activity, wait around during the event, and then drive everyone home. Still, my counsel is to volunteer yourself for carpool duty when possible. A mom hears so much in the car as the kids joke and talk about their everyday lives. It is surprising how often they forget that Mom is in the front seat, and they reveal enlightening truths. I have also found that having my desk next to our home's media center is a terrific source of knowledge. Even though it is distracting and noisy, a mom learns a lot from that vantage point.

It is crucial for families to develop ways of living that allow them to bond and serve as a way to further and strengthen familial bonds. Fishing, cooking, camping out—there are any number of ways to glue our families together. While we all enjoy Christmas it can sometimes feel more like a military maneuver than a holiday. The family Christmas picture, the decorations, and the caroling are great, but Christmas can get a bit overwhelming, especially with the rampant materialism of our culture. Of course we love the spiritual aspects of Christmas, but as a pure holiday our family prefers Thanksgiving when each family member participates in the kitchen cooking with me and sharing great memories of Thanksgivings gone by.

Both Gregory and I came from families where our best times as families were while traveling. Our best selves came out to play and no surprise, Gregory and I travel a great deal with our children, and we all love it. To this day, all our kids, even the ones in their twenties, ask excitedly, "Where are we going for summer vacation this year?" I am quite sure that our children will replicate our example of hospitality and vacation with their own families in the future. Everyone wants to recreate that which was happy in his or her own childhood.

THE DANGERS OF THE ELECTRONIC WORLD

A potential danger facing families today is that while we are more connected electronically, we can be more disconnected personally. Social media and the electronic world can act as a hindrance to communication. In our experience, boys tend to get sucked into video and computer games, and girls can be consumed by social media. Their electronic world can suck up so much of their attention that they can easily become numb to real human interactions. I had a visceral reaction the first time one of our children interrupted me midsentence to answer the cell phone at dinner. Since then, we have made sure our children know proper cell phone etiquette. Our job as parents is to keep our kids connected to us and not to allow technology to replace human interaction. On the other hand, I do love the convenience and safety the new technology can bring to our families. A flat tire or a pickup at school can be dealt with by an easy phone call. Technology is our friend if we harness it. We cannot let it run wild and control our families.

In a research study by Kleiner Perkins Caufield Byers, it was noted that the average cell phone user checks his or her phone 150 times a day.[2] In another study entitled "Pulling off the Mask: The Impact of Social Networking Activities on Evangelical Christian College Students" by Gordon College in Massachusetts, it was reported that some students spend as much as fifty hours per week on social media pursuits, and that does not include talking on the phone or watching TV.[3] YouTube, Netflix, Facebook, and the Internet make it easy not only to waste time, but this obsessive usage also dampens community building to a striking degree.

Moms will see much less electronic use if we keep our kids connected and in community. Internet and electronic addiction is a very real problem. It can stifle the spiritual growth of our children and kill the family dynamic. Kids need to learn how to spend the day productively apart from electronics, and they should be steered to satisfying activities and entertainment. Kids use electronics to feel connected with their peers and with the larger world. Learning to use social media responsibly is the answer. We have to help our kids make wise choices about how to spend their time. We do this in part by helping them learn to value community and family time. There is no substitute for interacting with real people.

COLLECTIVE WISDOM

I love to garden. When I garden I feel close to my father since he had such talent with flowers. I fell in love with our New Hampshire home when I saw the beautifully entwined vines of the wisteria wrapping their thick roots on columns the length of the house. Hanover's landscape while quite beautiful with its maples and elms does not boast much variety. Everywhere I looked, I saw the same trees, plants, and shrubs.

I had no gardening experience in the far north. Counsel from new friends, the town's gardening club, and the local nursery would have protected me from some very expensive mistakes. In the years we have lived here, we have experienced weather that ranged from thirty below zero Fahrenheit to one hundred above in the same year. We have had summers of drought when the plants wilted, and summers when it rained for days and the flowers grew moldy and limp. We have had deer and groundhogs chew up the gorgeous flowers. Within two years of moving to Hanover, I learned to ask questions from experienced, local gardeners to avoid crucial mistakes stemming from ignorance.

I know most women don't think they know it all in terms of wisdom; most of us, however, think that we *should* know it all. At least we feel we should have everything under control, which makes us shy away from asking advice and seeking counsel. In direct and honest conversations, we have to humble ourselves and admit things are not perfect. When that relates to our children, it is particularly painful. Being humble is essential as we seek advice and counsel. In the face of the brokenness in my life, it has been wise counsel that many times put me back on the path of grace.

My good friend Amy likes being independent and self-sufficient. Asking for help has always been uncomfortable to Amy. She does not like bothering others with her own concerns. But through a difficult family situation, Amy learned to turn to her church community and friends for help. She realized that she does not have to feel ashamed because we all need help at certain points in our lives. The Scriptures teach that it is in giving that we receive. So we are actually giving others an opportunity to be blessed by serving someone in need. Just be sure that when you have opportunities to serve others you do everything you can to help. We need each other.

In the book of Proverbs there are many verses that speak to the benefits that flow from collective wisdom such as: "Wisdom is found in those who take advice" (Prov. 13:10). Not only wisdom, but even victory comes from the counsel of many. I have been blessed with friends who are great mothers. I am thankful to have deeply spiritual friends who pray with me in the tough times and point me in the right direction. Remember this when you are looking for direction:

Plans fail for lack of counsel,
but with many advisers they succeed. (Prov. 15:22)

Do you have a group of women who speak into your life and the life of your family? Are you giving permission to allow these women to be "speaking the truth in love" (Eph. 4:15)? Have you built a community around your family that can support you through the tough times? It is vital to have the support of those who have gone before us, and in turn, we can help those who will come after us.

AVOID THE ECHO CHAMBER

Conversations among women can too easily become an echo chamber. In a philosophy class at Amherst College I was highly impressed by Jean-Paul Sartre's influential essay, "On Being and Nothingness." The salient point I took away from his essay is the human tendency to seek advice from someone who will simply confirm what we want to hear. It is important that we don't create an echo chamber because we are afraid to hear the truth. If you are only hearing from a small group of counselors who mirror back to you what you want to hear—or only what you have heard before—you will be hindered in your spiritual and emotional growth.

Moms can be vulnerable to needing only affirmation. We need to have husbands, friends, and wise counselors who are not afraid to tell us the truth. It is possible to lose friends over the issue of truth telling. While we cannot control how others receive counsel, we must be humble in our willingness to hear another's perspective. If someone comes to you about your child, don't turn that person away in a huff. Both Gregory and I are grateful when other adults come to us about our children. I don't mean gossip, which is toxic, but real facts that as parents we need to be aware of. Don't be one of those parents other adults are afraid to approach. Gregory and I learned that the daughter of one of our family friends was selling drugs to support her own drug habit. We told our friends what we knew, but sadly, they were in denial and didn't want to hear the truth.

We have been on the receiving end of difficult truths. It's hard on so many levels, but this is what we pray: "Lord, reveal to us what our children are doing, no matter how difficult. Let us be the first—not the last—to know." Once, an adult acquaintance approached Gregory with some painful information she had gleaned from Facebook (yes, it pays to check your child's Facebook pages and all their other electronic accounts) about one of our children. She was apologetic, and Gregory said she looked nervous, but we were grateful for the information regarding our child. Gregory and I keep praying that we know what our kids are doing. God answers these prayers. The truth is always our friend, even when it hurts.

COMMUNITY IS CRITICAL

Moms, dads, and their children form their own little community, but it is vital that we are connected to the larger community around us. It takes hard work for many of us to build communities of support around us. If we come from loving extended families, we will be blessed with a built-in support system from which we will draw strength our entire lives. Through many moves, Gregory and I have worked hard on building, and keeping, our most important friendships. Local churches have been a source of support, as have Bible studies and prayer groups. We must find community if we are to benefit from the collective wisdom we need to be the best moms we can be. Obviously jobs are an important source of friendships, as are athletic programs (our own and our kids'), schools, and volunteer positions. While all this may seem obvious, research tells us that a growing portion of our population is very lonely. Community building is essential to human joy, and as moms we are in a critical position as community builders.

One of the beauties of reading the Word of God is that we are entering the community of those who have lived out their lives in the pursuit of the Lord. The Lord brings us into His community and speaks freshly into our lives via His Word. We need that as mothers, and as women. Do not forsake the community of the Word—it will feed you, it will surprise you, and it will challenge you with a continually new way of seeing the world.

We cannot have a strong, spiritual anchor in this world without that living relationship to the Word and to others. When we read, we are receiving wise counsel. At the same time, we have been created to be intimately connected to others.

The Bible warns us that people who isolate themselves are in danger of selfishness and foolishness. As it is written in Proverbs 18:1:

> A man who isolates himself seeks his own desire;
> he rages against all wise judgment. (NKJV)

Today this growing trend of isolated and lonely adults can be fatal to families, for none of us was meant to be alone.

PLAY DATES

My mother said something very wise to me as the kids were growing up. I was feeling quite disappointed that my young children were not being invited to their friends' homes very much. She said that it actually was better to have play dates at our house because I knew what I allowed in my home. That was profound wisdom. Now that I have children well into their twenties, I am thankful that I stepped up to the plate and extended myself in play dates, even when there was no quid pro quo. Sure, some neighborhood moms took advantage of our open door policy by pawning their kids off on us. But for our kids, and for their friends, it was a true blessing because it helped them form community. In the end, that is all that matters.

When I was growing up, all the kids in my neighborhood played on the street. We had street fairs, directed plays, and our mothers simply told us on summer nights to be back home at 8 p.m. Streets were safe and served as playgrounds for hopscotch and kickball. Kids were not sent off to camps, tennis lessons, and all the other things we create for our kids today so that they are active and safe. Even stay-at-home moms have to opt into extracurricular activities to some extent. I did this so my children would not be lonely—when all the neighborhood kids are locked into busy schedules and close friends are committed to their activities, it becomes a case of when in Rome, do as the Romans do.

A clear-headed strategy of being ground zero for your kids and their friends will not only protect your kids in the long run, but it will save you as a mom from resentment. When I realized that this was part of God's plan for me, I was able to see it as a privilege in mentoring the next generation beyond my own kids. I came to realize that being hospitable to my children's friends was part of my greater ministry, and this has ultimately brought me great joy.

From California to Virginia to Bermuda to New Hampshire, we have always kept an open door policy because we know what we allow—and what we don't. I am around during the day feeding the starving hordes—food is a great initiator with kids. Many great conversations have begun over a plate of cookies. Our house has become a magnet for those kids who have nowhere else to go. When we have hosted parties for teenagers, either Gregory or I are at the door greeting our young guests and we stay up, even to the early hours of the morning, to monitor everyone and to say good night. Kids need outlets, and if we don't do the work and provide entertainment that we can control, they will look for it elsewhere. After all, our children are created to be social creatures just as we are.

As with everything else, building community requires wisdom. A friendship that begins at age five may not stand the test of time. It is difficult to close the proverbial door to young kids for whom one feels love and concern. Yet we have come to the conclusion that for the sake of our kids there are times when friendships need to be pruned. In these rare but important situations, I have found our kids usually have some understanding that all is not right in that friendship. Frequently they have been relieved when we have taken the responsibility of curtailing an unhealthy relationship.

Ultimately, the three Cs of motherhood are about the ministry of relationships and how we can build them to be healthy and vibrant. Jesus wants us to prioritize relationships because that is what He did in His ministry on earth, and He continues to do so from His throne in heaven. He was not only the Christ, Jesus was also the first Christian. He lived out His life on earth to show us how it's done. As moms, the ministry of Jesus is such a comfort, because in a way, He came to mother His people: "How often I have longed to gather your children together, as a hen gathers her chicks under her wings" (Matt. 23:37). Let us therefore continue our motherly ministry to our families and our communities, knowing the Lord is with us in this good work.

Ponder

God's Word

Be still, and know that I am God. (Ps. 46:10)

Wisdom is found in those who take advice. (Prov. 13:10)

Now you are the body of Christ, and each one of you is a part of it. (1 Cor. 12:27)

Plans fail for lack of counsel,
but with many advisers they succeed. (Prov. 15:22)

The Authors' Words

"Our children need to know that when they confess their failings to us we are listening first, and we will then act according to our great love and respect for them."

Assess

1. The authors list several places that lend themselves to listening to your children: the kitchen, the dinner table (no cell phones!), car rides, and vacations. What works for you? Can you add others to this list?
2. Do you have any friends who love you enough to tell you the truth, or do you seek an echo chamber? What kind of friend are you to others?
3. Why is it important that your home be a center of community for your children's friends? How could you move toward that goal?

4. Do you seek out wise friends who can give you good input, even if it is at times contrary to your own ways of thinking or acting? And are you open and receptive to these ideas?
5. Do your children come to you to share with you their deepest concerns and biggest mistakes? If not, why not? What can you do to help build a deeper level of communication and trust?

Sum Up

Moms are in a dialogue and not a monologue. Being a mom means being in conversation. We are engaged in conversations with our spouse, our children, our community, our church, and our God. We get so much wisdom and joy from others, so take the time to cultivate these conversations and really listen to what you hear.

Ten

Parenting in the Age of Busy: Time Is Our Friend

The Internet is an interesting place to pick up parenting stories. One story that went viral in the spring of 2014 is entitled "The Day I Left My Son in the Car" on Salon.com. Kim Brooks is the author, and she starts off with a passage that every parent I know can relate to: "The day it happened was no different from most; I was worried and I was running late. I was worried because in a few hours' time I was going to be enduring a two and a half hour flight with my kids, ages 1 to 4. I was running late because, like many parents of small children, I often find there just aren't enough hours in the day."[1]

Because Ms. Brooks was running around getting ready for the plane trip back home after a visit to her mom, she left her son in her mother's car unattended while she ran into the store for five minutes to pick up something that would amuse her son on the plane. A bystander noticed the little boy alone in the car, whipped out his iPhone, called 911, and shot a video. The police traced the car to Ms. Brooks's mom and ended up issuing Ms. Brooks a warrant of arrest.

I think we can all relate to a frazzled day that causes us to make human errors in judgment. Gregory and I had three children in three and a half years, and I dreaded our frequent plane trips, with me often alone traveling with the babies. I cursed the planes for making the stewards' call button an enticing orange, and I frequently batted down plump hands reaching for it, not always successfully. So I read Ms. Brooks's story with empathy because I can easily relate to the stress of feeling overwhelmed as a mom. But what I found most interesting is that in her concern to justify herself and to reassure both herself and the reader that she is a very safety-conscious mom, she did not once mention the most important thing: she loves her son. Not once. I counted the times she even used the word *love*, and it was rarely used and never in conjunction with her kids. This reflects the salient fact that being busy can often drown out what is most important in life, namely, loving our kids. In the hustle and bustle of life, our heavenly Father does not want busyness to drown out what's most important. In fact, He wants to help us make time our friend in every area of our lives.

THE TYRANNY OF THE TRIVIAL

Being busy is a reality every mom must contend with, but we have to recognize that busyness often interferes with essential long-term goals for our families. It is crucial that love for our family triumph over what I call the tyranny of the trivial. With so many things calling for our urgent attention, we can all too easily take our eyes off what truly matters. If we are not careful, the glossing over what is truly important to get the details of life attended to can grow into a bad habit with long-term, unintended consequences.

For example, when my children were very young, it was hard to get up early enough in the morning to have my quiet time with God. Before I had children, I devoted an hour each day to read the Scriptures and to pray. But once I had babies, I discovered that no matter how early I got up, the kids woke up earlier. And once they woke up, there was precious little time and almost no quiet. For several years I fell into a pattern of not having quiet time. At the end of the night, all I wanted to do was have some "me" time. I have never been an individual who found it necessary to have my entire day jam-packed. I like being by myself to contemplate and think. This really helped me in my spiritual life before we had kids. But once we had them, life quickly got so busy it seemed I didn't have time to interact with anyone— even the Lord. It took me a long time to realize I was crowding out God to attend to everyone and everything else. I now have brought back with conscious deliberateness a steady pattern of spiritual disciplines without which I cannot grow in faith.

Life as a mom brings with it the peril of great lists of things to get done. Busyness can be a trap that causes us to lose touch with God, our families, and even with our own souls. Over time, busyness can sap us of joy and purpose that connectedness brings. These dangers are very real for all of us, especially young mothers. As young moms we wake up to the sounds of children's voices calling for our attention. We might not have gotten a full night of sleep. We attend to the physical needs of the kids. If we are employed outside the home, we set up the day for the caregiver; if we are homemakers we set our kids to productive activities. Each day revolves around tasks and details. In the evening everyone looks to us for dinner. By the time evening comes, we are usually dead-tired. We only want to read a good book or watch a movie and then go to sleep. I know this reality all too well, for I have lived it.

This trap of busy is set for everyone. Most of the things we are doing for our families fall under the categories of "good" or "important." Choosing what to cut back on in order to spend some quality time with the Lord, with our spouse, and with our kids is difficult. Should we cut back on something as worthwhile as supporting our church or schools through a bake sale or something as important as doing my job outside the house? Our families need us to do most of the things we are committed to. They benefit from our commitments. But all together, they set a pace and a schedule that, for many of us, is overwhelming.

All the doing can separate us from being our heavenly Father's beloved daughters and from enjoying His presence and His love daily. These times of refreshing allow us to fill up the empty cisterns in our soul. Jesus gives us a perfect illustration of this when He was talking with another mother, the Samaritan woman at the well in John 4:14: "whoever drinks the water I give them will never thirst. Indeed, the water I give them will become in them a spring of water welling up to eternal life."

Not only does the Lord fill our own emptiness, but He promises to fill us to overflowing so that we might fill others. It is precisely by being full of His rivers of living water that we can take from our fullness and in turn give love and peace to our own families. It is all too easy to go through a string of days and weeks when we don't enjoy times of refreshing with the Lord. Being too busy is dangerous for both us and for our families. Burnout is the end state of too busy for too long. Burnout is the exact opposite of where the Lord wants us to be.

COUNTERING THE CULTURE OF BUSYNESS

So how do we counter our culture of busyness, a pattern that runs deeply in so many of us? The first thing we must remember is this: time is our friend. Our heavenly Father created time, and He gives it freely to each one of us. Time is not the enemy in our lives, although I often live as if it were: *Oh, if only I had more time, I could accomplish . . .* But God is not worried about time because He created it in order to unfold His eternal plan. It is a false way of seeing things when we believe Plan B is in play because somehow Plan A was derailed. Living patiently is what God requires. I know it does not help to add anxiety to the mix because I am in such a hurry.

We have exactly the same gift every single day: twenty-four hours to invest as we choose. So if time is our friend, how can we manage it in a way that honors our heavenly Father and enables us to take care of those He has given us? How do we really make time our friend? I have learned several important lessons from some of the best moms I know. The first and most important lesson is this: find time to sit at Jesus' feet and be refreshed by His Spirit. The Gospel of Luke's story about Mary and Martha is truly insightful. Martha is just like most of us today: hardworking, taking care of everyone, and a bit upset that others aren't helping out. In fact, she implicitly criticizes her sister Mary for not helping, a fair criticism on the face of it. But Jesus has a surprising answer for Martha, one that can help us if we take time to understand and put into practice: "Martha, Martha . . . you are worried and upset about many things, but few things are needed—or indeed only one. Mary has chosen what is better, and it will not be taken away from her" (Luke 10:41–42).

Notice how tenderly Jesus addresses Martha. He's not mad at her. He understands what she is doing and why she is doing it. It is comforting for us to know that the Lord understands what we are doing and why we are doing it. But Jesus doesn't stop there; He wants Martha to be freed by the truth. The truth is that Martha is worried and upset about things that in the long run don't matter very much. It's not that serving others isn't important; Jesus told us that He Himself came "not . . . to be served, but to serve" (Mark 10:45). Martha's problem was one of priorities. She could have spent a beautiful time of refreshing with the Lord and done the housework later. Because there is always more housework.

Mary made the wiser choice. She chose to sit at Jesus' feet while she could. She wanted to learn from His wisdom and to be refreshed by His Spirit. I know being with Jesus is something I need on a regular basis. There is no substitute for time with Jesus. One more note on this great story: in Jewish culture at that time, only male disciples could sit at the very feet of the Master. But Mary did it anyway, which clearly pleased Jesus. We need to be bold like Mary and sit at His proverbial feet every chance we get.

Of course different women enjoy and experience refreshing times with Christ in many ways. Some of us love to worship the Lord in praise. Some love to dig into the Word and ask our Father to speak to us through His Holy Spirit. Others get the most out of being with a small group of friends who are committed to each other and meet regularly to pray and read the Word. Still others simply love to pray and spend time with the Lord in the beauty of nature. None of these are better or more spiritual than the others. We must each find the ways that are most meaningful for us personally.

THE STORY OF SUSANNA WESLEY: MAKING DAILY TIME WITH THE LORD

A key issue for moms is finding the time on a regular basis to sit at the Lord's feet. While this is not easy for any of us, it can be particularly challenging for young mothers. We can study the life of Susanna Wesley, the mother of John and Charles Wesley, to see the impact that spending time with God can have on the lives of our children. John and Charles Wesley were two of the most influential Christians of the eighteenth century. John founded the Methodist Church and launched one of the greatest revivals in Anglo-American history. Charles, an influential writer, wrote many Christian hymns that we still sing today. Their mother was a tremendous influence on these godly men.

Susanna Wesley was left virtually impoverished by her husband, who was rarely at home. She had nineteen children, ten of whom survived into adulthood. Susanna raised them, educated them, and provided for them by herself, all in a modest cottage with no modern conveniences. It must have been hard for her to find time to sit at the Lord's feet every day. Yet she did, and she did so in a way that taught her children both a profound respect for the Lord and the importance of spending time with Him daily.

Susanna Wesley had a habit we could profit from today in our busy world. Every evening at roughly the same time she would take her Bible and sit in her favorite chair with a blanket draped around her. This was a strict sign that she was not to be disturbed. The older children understood that during these periods they were to take care of the younger children without bothering Mom because she was sitting at Jesus' feet. During these times, Susanna would worship, read the Word, pray, and meditate. She would enjoy time with our Lord. Her children remarked that her eyes often sparkled when she was finished. She credited her daily time with Jesus as giving her the wisdom, the love, and the strength she needed to raise up her children. It also gave her time each day to ask the Lord's direct blessing on her children and His help in all the challenges that were too big for her to handle alone.

I'm not suggesting that we have to be just like Susanna Wesley with our Bible, rocking chair, and blanket. But her example speaks to us today across the years. I know I want to have a fresh dose of the Lord's wisdom and strength, and I need to be willing to make the time. I have to force myself to turn off the electronics, stop answering e-mail, and spend time with God. As moms we must be willing to cut back on the housework or to tell our boss that we cannot take on that extra project. These choices are not easy, and many times the cost of these choices is high indeed. By inviting Jesus to commune with us, however, we will learn the truth that time is indeed our friend, not our enemy.

We moms are busy. I know that. But I still want to encourage you to set a time to sit at His feet every day. Ask the Holy Spirit to show you His way. Read and study His Word and it will come alive to you and guide you. One of the most salient aspects of the virtuous woman in Proverbs 31 is that "she speaks with wisdom, and faithful instruction is on her tongue" (v. 26). As you raise your children to be wise and virtuous, you will find yourself referencing the Word as you instruct them. We as mothers may plan our steps, but He guides our path. We will only fully comprehend the depth of guidance through knowledge of the Word. Wise moms are connected to the Word by the Spirit. And that only happens with time.

RELATIONSHIPS ARE ETERNAL

There is a second important lesson I have learned to make time truly my friend and it is this: relationships are what really matter. Our relationships—especially with family and our closest friends—will last into eternity. Nothing else will. Not our possessions or our degrees or our money or our fame. We take nothing with our immortal souls into eternity except the relationships we form here on earth. I have learned not to skimp on what I value most: my relationships with God, my family, and my friends.

Many of us do not even have time to deal with the blessings, let alone the inevitable struggles that come to all families. Things get swept under the rug, not because we don't love our kids or that we are lazy, but simply because we don't have the time to deal with one more thing. But leaving our kids to their own devices because we are too harried, too distracted, or too exhausted will not bring the harvest we desire. Nor will it build the deep, loving, respectful relationships that we all want to have with our children when they are grown. If we do not spend large amounts of time with our children when they are young, they may never develop the security and sense of self-worth they need to be fully functioning, productive adults.

We knew a wonderful couple in the early years of our marriage. The husband was busily pursuing a doctorate, working full time, raising four children with his lovely wife, and coaching little league in his "free" time. He and his wife are God-fearing, faithful people who truly love the Lord. Sadly, their older sons have struggled with deeply troubled personal lives. However, their youngest girls are bright and happy and are serving the Lord. The daughters are younger by more than ten years. What is the difference?

It seems to me that these wonderful people were just too busy in the early part of the childrearing years. Too many things were overlooked in the mad rush to maintain their crazy schedules. Then a few years later, they went to live in a very conservative country. Both the girls and the parents had fewer opportunities for outside activities. This meant our friends spent much more time with their daughters, whom they homeschooled. All the time together had a very positive impact on the children. Same parents, same commitment to the Lord, same love for each of their children. But when the hyperactivity of affluent America was substituted for a more family-oriented life in a relatively poor country, the children thrived. No little league, no ballet lessons, but the fruit has been terrific.

This example has influenced our choices in our own home. We realized that all the activities we want to be involved with could serve as a stumbling block to having the kind of family we want. We are very careful, not only for us but also for our children, in the activities we commit to. Fun, fascinating endeavors are terrific. But if our involvement has a detrimental impact on the time we spend with the kids, Gregory and I will put the family first. We purposed to invest in large amounts of time with our children, and it has been the single best investment we have ever made.

Like daily times of refreshing with the Lord, making time every day to be with members of your family is a source of blessing and refreshment for them and for you. And like our daily times of refreshing with Jesus, quality time with family doesn't happen by accident. You must plan for it and help make it happen. Whether it is family dinners together or going somewhere fun on the weekend, or even watching a family movie together . . . plan it and do it. There is no better return on investment than the time you spend with your kids, both now and in the future.

Be sure to plan some one-on-one time every day with each of your kids: even if it is just reading a story at night or praying with each as he or she wakes up, driving each to his or her sports practice or taking a short walk together. Each of our children needs a personal relationship with us. The only way to develop a strong personal relationship is by spending time with each other, both with the entire family and also one on one. From their personal relationship with you, your children will develop a strong sense of self-worth and self-confidence (*I am lovable because I am loved*). It also enables them to trust others and develop lifelong friendships, which is a third way of making time our friend.

MAKING TIME FOR LIFELONG FRIENDSHIPS

How many of us have lifelong friends today? Research tells us that the number of American men who report that they have no real friends has increased dramatically in the past thirty years.[2]

We all know that men generally have a harder time forming deep friendships, but a similar trend is impacting women. It's not hard to see that one of the causes of this very negative social dynamic is again, busyness.

All of us need a few true friends. God made us to be social creatures. But today's high-pressured, super-technological world allows us to substitute Facebook acquaintances for friendships. Electronic acquaintances come and go with little time invested or real commitment from either side. True friendships, while time-consuming, are tremendous sources of joy, comfort, and stability in our unstable world.

So how do we go about making time our friend by building lifelong friendships? For some people like my husband, this seems as natural as breathing. For others, it is just the opposite. But for all of us, one of the keys to building true lifelong friendships is investing time in the right way with the people God has placed in our lives.

Spending time with other moms who love Jesus is a wise investment of time. Spending time with a few older women who can provide wise counsel and needed encouragement can be a great investment of time. If you're an experienced mom, consider mentoring younger moms. Mentoring younger moms is an important part of our ministry and a beautiful and life-giving investment into their lives.

Lifelong friendships are rarely chosen up front. Friendships tend to develop over time, out of common values, passions, and commitments. But the key ingredient to any lifelong friendship is quality time together. Make time your friend by investing your friendship time with other women who share your values, passions, and commitments. Be sure to go deep; don't just stay on the surface. Thomas Aquinas wrote, "There is nothing on this earth more to be prized than true friendship."

Jesus was an insignificant carpenter born in the middle of nowhere. He was never harried, never rushed, but He ministered to thousands. He made time for the relationships that really mattered. He cared deeply about His heavenly Father, His family, and His friends. It was with them that He invested His life. It was through these relationships that He changed the world. Jesus' life is an example to us. Our bowing down to the tyranny of the trivial does not accomplish His will. I want to be like Mary. I want Jesus to be my friend who speaks into my life. I want to be found sitting at Jesus' feet.

Ponder

God's Word

Whoever drinks the water I give them will never thirst. Indeed, the water I give them will become in them a spring of water welling up to eternal life. (John 4:14)

Martha, Martha . . . you are worried and upset about many things, but few things are needed—or indeed only one. Mary has chosen what is better, and it will not be taken away from her. (Luke 10:41–42)

For Yours is the kingdom and the power and the glory forever. (Matt. 6:13 NKJV)

The Authors' Words

"[Our heavenly Father] wants to help us make time our friend in every area of our lives."

Assess

1. In your own life, where can you go or what can you do to find time to drink of God's living water? Be as practical as possible.
2. Why is one-on-one time so important for your children? How can you work more of it into your family's lifestyle?
3. Think of at least one "good thing" that is keeping you so busy that you are missing time to build relationships. How can you escape this trap?

4. How can we see time as a friend when the clock seems like an enemy? What specific steps can you take to make time your friend?
5. Are you spending quality time (almost) every day with your heavenly Father? With your spouse? With your children? If not, why not? What can you do to establish those positive, life-giving patterns?

Sum Up

So much to do, so little time to do it in. In our society, we mostly think of time as our enemy. But God created time, and He is in control. Surrendering the stress of time is liberating and life changing. As a good friend says, a day of His favor is better than a year of our labor.

Eleven

Wisdom for Single Moms: Hope Is Available

The statistics are striking: last year twelve million families in America were headed by a single parent, the vast majority of whom are moms. In the industrialized world, almost 16 percent of kids live in single parent households.[1] I don't think most women dream of heading their own families, yet this reality has hit our generation very hard. While there is something innately strengthening in partnership, we know that God can and does minister His grace and wisdom to single moms. I am very grateful to several close single-mother friends who have helped craft this chapter since I have never experienced being a single parent. We all hope and pray that single moms will be strengthened and encouraged through it.

LYDIA'S STORY

The first life history I would like to share is from the perspective of a woman who was raised by a single mom in the 1960s. Lydia grew up in a family with no father. Lydia never even met her dad. Her mom was a faithful woman who instilled in her kids a strong work ethic, patriotism, and most importantly, faith. Lydia grew up with very little money, but this ended up being to her benefit since it served as important preparation for her life's work, being a missionary. She learned early on not to place a high priority on material possessions. Her family rarely purchased brand-name clothes or shoes. Her mom never had much, but she loved her kids and did everything she could to support them. Kids really want a loving and giving family with fewer possessions than to own everything and live in a family where love is absent.

Lydia's mom did have times of trouble making ends meet, but they were blessed with help from the maternal grandparents and from living in a small Texas community with caring neighbors. Lydia's mom worked at the local five and dime. Lydia and her siblings started work early on paper routes, mowing lawns, and babysitting to contribute to the family income.

Lydia never really understood the reason for her parents' breakup. But she has always appreciated that her mom refrained from criticizing her absent dad. Lydia's mom never once made her feud with her dad into Lydia's feud. Lydia knows that she was very blessed to have her maternal grandfather around every day to be a great role model. She never heard anything negative from her grandparents about her dad. When she was old enough to ask questions, her mom and grandparents were open enough, although discreet in the particulars. Their attitude helped Lydia to deal with the truth, but at the same time not to feel abandoned or alone. Lydia and her siblings have all gone into Christian ministry and have built healthy, thriving marriages and families. Lydia feels that integral to her story is the forgiveness that flowed in the family. Her mom's forgiveness helped defeat the generational curse that divorce can so easily become.

TRACY'S STORY

Tracy's parents got married in their thirties after they had both established their careers and their lives. They felt a great deal of resentment toward the restrictions that marriage brought to them. By the time Tracy was five, her parents could barely talk to each other without erupting into a fight. By the time she was ten, they preferred not to talk at all. Finally, they sought a divorce when Tracy was in high school. Both Tracy and her brother were mostly left to fend for themselves during the holidays and vacations since their parents were on to new partners and new pursuits. Her parents were focused on fulfilling themselves, as many in our culture urge us to do.

Tracy really struggled after college landing a job. She had found no mentor, and her parents were too busy for her. Tracy's brother got into heavy drug use and is now in an institution. Tracy came to faith, but the wounds she brought into her first marriage caused her to at first ignore the problems with her husband and then abandon the marriage when things got tough. She is now of the opinion that she could have changed the course of her first marriage if only she knew how. Her first husband was a decent man who himself was the product of divorce. There had been no abuse or adultery, and Tracy regrets her inability in establishing a healthy functioning relationship with him.

Tracy is currently divorcing her second husband. He, too, has nothing truly wrong with him, but Tracy is finding the daily commitment needed in marriage is beyond her capacity, or at least she "feels" this way. Tracy's parents gave into their feelings, and they have doomed their daughter to repeat their mistakes. The greatest tragedy of a family is when the parents misguidedly live their lives to the exclusion of what is best for their children. Almost always in those cases everyone loses.

JOAN'S STORY

Joan never imagined that she would be a divorced, single parent. Her strict Chinese upbringing had steered her toward overachievement, and she was accustomed to succeeding at the goals she had set for herself. She earned a bachelor's degree from Stanford and went on to earn a master's in business administration at the University of California, Berkeley. Her background and all her accomplishments did not prepare her for motherhood. Nothing prepared her for the moment when her husband told her that he didn't love her anymore and he wanted a divorce. When she found herself as a single mom through divorce she was devastated. In this long and difficult journey, she had learned a great deal about motherhood, dashed dreams, and God's great grace.

During her pregnancy, Joan had pictured raising a child in a family with two loving parents and being a happy mother and wife. In thirty seconds that picture was shattered. When Abby was six months old, Ted moved out of the house. The legal process took time, and for the next three years she and Ted went to counseling to try to reconcile their differences but were ultimately unsuccessful. The divorce was finalized when Abby was four years old.

Financially, Joan was in a good situation. Many single moms have to cope with the urgent and extremely stressful issues of child care and limited resources. She was grateful that she was able to hire a nanny to help care for Abby. She was a wonderful caretaker and a great source of comfort to Joan as she walked through the pain of separation and divorce. She learned from the nanny how to physically care for Abby as an infant and toddler. Caring for a baby did not come easily to Joan. It was a struggle for her to take care of Abby's physical needs, especially when she was fighting to stay afloat emotionally.

THE URGENT REQUIREMENT
OF FORGIVENESS

Joan's emotions ran the gamut: from fear that she would not be able to care for her child to anger and bitterness toward Ted for abandoning her and wanting to date other women. She knew that expressions of bitterness toward Ted in Abby's presence would be damaging to Abby. But at times she was unable to control her emotions when she interacted with Ted. It is often said that harboring bitterness is like drinking poison and expecting the other person to die. Though Joan knew that she was called to forgive, she was unable to come to the point of truly forgiving her ex-husband. She tried hard, she prayed, and she confessed her sin of unforgiveness to her spiritual mentors, but she just could not find it within herself to fully forgive Ted. She needed to go deeper and further in faith than she had ever done before. Her brokenness stood in the way of allowing her heavenly Father's help to do so.

God honored the deep cry of Joan's heart for the power to forgive. The Lord is able to use many different means to help us get where we need to go emotionally. Joan's help came in the form of a movie she watched entitled *The Passion of the Christ*. This movie depicts the story of Jesus' death on the cross in order to pay the price for our wrongdoing. Jesus had done nothing wrong, but even His closest friends abandoned Him. He absolutely did not deserve any part of the horrific treatment He received. As He was dying on the cross, instead of hating or cursing those who had abused Him so badly, Jesus blessed and forgave them: "Father, forgive them, for they do not know what they are doing" (Luke 23:34).

Jesus' words and reaction struck Joan hard: Who was she to not forgive Ted, when Jesus had willingly suffered a violent death on the cross to forgive her of all of her wrongdoing and sins? Jesus specifically asked her to do so in the Lord's Prayer:

> And forgive us our debts,
> as we also have forgiven our debtors. (Matt. 6:12)

At that moment, she inwardly bowed before the Lord and chose to let go of her bitterness toward Ted. She felt a deep release and knew a breakthrough had just happened, that a lasting forgiveness was birthed in her.

Forgiveness is a choice. It is a choice centered on letting go of rights, letting go of the desire to show the other person how wrong his or her actions were, and letting go of the desire to make the other person pay for his or her actions. Through the gift of God's forgiveness of her own sin, and by His grace and power, she was finally able to forgive Ted. She sensed a huge burden lifted, and the bitterness and anger that had dominated her interactions with Ted were released. Getting rid of the bitterness and anger freed her to become a more nurturing, compassionate, and loving mother for Abby.

Forgiveness is an ongoing process. It is all too easy to think back on the wrongdoings the other person committed and return to bitterness. It is also easy when new problems and disagreements arise to become angry again, allowing bitterness to take new root. Jesus taught us that forgiveness is a lifelong process (Matt. 18:22), knowing that new difficulties and temptations will continually arise. But He gives us the power to forgive again and again, to get rid of the poison of bitterness and to have it replaced by His life-giving Spirit.

Other divorced friends we know have not chosen to embrace forgiveness. The impact on their children—and on their own relationships—has been devastating. Do not underestimate the power of bitterness to poison your own heart and all that you hold dear. Don't swallow that poison.

OVERCOMING DIFFERENCES IN PARENTING

At times, Joan wished that she was the only parent raising Abby, who is now a teenager. Ted and she have joint custody, so he spends a great deal of time with Abby. They have widely differing views on parenting, and Joan resents the negative influences she believes Ted allows too easily (lurid TV programs, music with inappropriate lyrics, a disrespectful attitude and tone of voice, and so on). Most parents struggle with differing opinions in various areas of parenting, but divorce magnifies the differences and there is often less commonality as the years go by. For many years, Ted and Joan could not agree on a unified approach to many aspects of parenting: setting boundaries, disciplining, and allowing media influences were all areas of conflict. They each parented Abby according to their own values and standards. She felt that her effectiveness as a parent was constantly being sabotaged. Joan would make progress with Abby in certain areas that Ted either did not agree with or did not care about, and then Abby would regress after spending time with her father.

COUNSELING AND THE NEED FOR COMMUNITY AND MENTORS

Looking back on those earlier years of coparenting, Joan is grateful that one course of action Ted and she both agreed upon was seeking the help of a marriage and family therapy counselor. They took the time to find a good counselor, knowing that there are lots of bad ones out there, and went to regularly scheduled appointments to discuss their differences in parenting. Their counselor had a positive role in helping Joan and Ted better understand each other's viewpoint. They also agreed to put Abby's needs first and foremost in their discussions. After fourteen years of coparenting Abby, Ted and Joan have come to a place where they can truly listen to and respect the other person's perspective. They can discuss the best strategy and course of action in parenting by putting Abby's interests first. This has been the key to successful parenting in a stressful situation.

As a divorced mother, Joan found that parenting solo can

be lonely and painful as one doesn't have the moral and emotional support of a spouse. However, one great blessing for which she is deeply grateful is the community of friends, mothers, and church members who have supported her. She has actively sought out the friendship and support of other mothers, and this has brought her great comfort and support through difficult times.

When Abby was eighteen months old, Joan found a "Mother and Me" class at a church near her home and started to meet regularly with other mothers and children. She became good friends with one of the mothers. Helen and Joan shared their hearts as moms, supported each other through challenging times, and their daughters have become close friends. She also joined another group of moms with children Abby's age, and those friendships have been another source of encouragement, wisdom, and comfort. One of the mothers, Sarah, has a son Abby's age and two older daughters. Sarah was also a leader in the church and in their community. Her quiet strength, loving concern, and wise advice have been great blessings and sources of comfort. In fact, Sarah became in effect an older sister for Joan. Through these friendships Joan has learned that there is no substitute for faithful prayers, true friendship, and wise counsel in her life as a mother.

Joan has always sought the wisdom of parents of children and young adults who exhibited exceptional moral character. We are parenting in very difficult times, where the cultural and media influences on children, teens, and young adults are powerful and very often destructive. The rates of teen suicide, drug and alcohol use, teen pregnancies, sexually transmitted diseases, anxiety, and depression have multiplied over the past two decades. The attitudes and values she observes in many teens and young adults today are attitudes and values that she does not want to see her daughter adopting. Joan carefully observed Abby's peers at school and other activities and sought the advice and wisdom of mothers of children who exhibited exceptional character.

She found that these mothers were always happy to share their wisdom and encouragement. Just their being honest with her about their struggles and difficulties in raising their own children was incredibly helpful. She felt comforted that she was not alone in dealing with parenting difficulties. It reassured her to learn that even the parents of the most exemplary children have challenging times in raising their children, teens, and young adults. This concept was surprising to her, as she grew up under traditional Chinese parenting, where her parents and their friends did not openly share struggles in parenting. Growing to understand that even the most experienced and wise mothers have real struggles was a great help and comfort to her.

LEARNING NEW METHODS OF PARENTING

Over the years, Joan read many good books and articles on parenting and attended classes and seminars on this subject. To be honest, it has been hard for her to put many of these teachings into practice. Some of the parenting techniques and strategies did prove to be helpful, but she found that she had a strong tendency to parent out of a default mode that was ingrained in her, largely from the way she herself was parented. She sensed that she needed to make some changes deep within herself to be a more effective mother to Abby and prayed that God would help her. In another class on the strategies and techniques of parenting, Joan came to realize that parenting is not a "task" (Joan had been treating it as such), but a journey in which we are learning and growing alongside our children. This insight helped Joan see some of the areas she needed to grow in, with God's help, to be a better mother to Abby.

One specific area was letting go of using fear, intimidation, anger, and control to try to get Abby to do what Joan thought was right. Joan learned that lasting change does not come from using such tactics. We only get involved with unfruitful rounds of discipline if we do not first lay the foundation of training in prayer. Joan began to pray to God about specific areas that she needed to discipline Abby in. She discovered that God would give her wisdom on how to approach Abby about a specific behavior or need and that Abby would be more receptive to her teaching and discipline.

GETTING YOUR EX-HUSBAND REALLY INVOLVED

There is no doubt this is one of the greatest challenges for many single moms. Joan's ex is now a very involved father, but many are not. Joan found early on that constant criticism and nagging had the opposite effect from what she had hoped. Interestingly enough, when she looked for opportunities to praise and thank Ted for good things he was doing as a father, he really took it to heart. Joan even bought Ted a copy of *Be a Better Dad Today*, which has an entire chapter devoted to divorced dads that urges dads to take their parental responsibilities seriously.[2]

Most men are more sensitive than you might think. Criticism, condemnation, and judgment are generally not successful tools when single moms want to encourage their exes to be present in their children's lives. Try praise and thanksgiving along with a dose of man-to-man encouragement from other committed dads. Joan found this method worked much better than negativity.

Joan's journey as a divorced single mother continues to be filled with challenges, pain, personal growth, and hope. Each day brings an opportunity to put into practice the wisdom she is learning. It is a joy for her to watch Abby grow to know that she has a Father in heaven; God Almighty is watching over her. Joan's journey as a single mom is far from over, but she has made great strides. Her daughter has directly benefited, and Joan herself has more peace and joy in her life. God's grace indeed.

Ponder

God's Word

Father, forgive them, for they do not know what they are doing. (Luke 23:34)

If any of you lacks wisdom, you should ask God, who gives generously to all without finding fault, and it will be given to you. (James 1:5)

In Him you also trusted, after you heard the word of truth, the gospel of your salvation; in whom also, having believed, you were sealed with the Holy Spirit of promise, who is the guarantee of our inheritance until the redemption of the purchased possession, to the praise of His glory. (Eph. 1:13–14 NKJV)

The Authors' Words

"Harboring bitterness is like drinking poison and expecting the other person to die."

Assess

1. Why is it so deadly to hold onto bitterness? Is this a problem for you?
2. When might it be best to seek professional help from a family counselor versus asking for help, advice, and support from your friends and church community? What are the advantages of each?

3. Are you seeking the help you need and deserve as a single mom?
4. Do you see parenting as a task or a journey? Or perhaps something else? Why?
5. What is your approach to your ex-husband? Is it one of criticism and judgment? If so, how is that working? What is your direction if your husband is abusive? And what if he is totally missing from the picture? Do you have the support you need?

Sum Up

Becoming a single mom does not change a mom's desire to be a good mom who raises her children well. God's wisdom and grace will lighten the burden of dashed dreams.

Twelve

Working Moms:
Excellence, Not Success

I
n a world where working moms are the norm, millions of women are trying to figure out the path to work–life balance. Many are looking for something or someone who will give them the silver bullet for what is an incredibly difficult task. The advice ranges from Facebook COO Sheryl Sandberg, who advocates that women "lean in" to their careers,[1] to a Washington Post article that sardonically suggests women "recline" into a less aggressive, less demanding, and more creative life.[2] You should just read some of the online comments on this debate!

As a mom, I have both worked from home and outside the home. I have consulted with great moms from both camps to get as many helpful insights as possible. Like many moms, I search for the answers to the ever-present questions of whether, where, and how I should work, and how I can manage to be a good mother at the same time. After nearly twenty-five years of struggling with these questions, I wish I could say there are "Ten Guaranteed Methods for Being a Successful Working Mom." Unfortunately, there are no quick and easy answers to this subject. What I can share with you are a few core things that good friends and I have learned along the way, sometimes the hard way. These are lessons that have helped me (and others) to find wholeness in this balancing of work and family, at least for a season. I hope and pray that they will be helpful to you as well.

One of the most important things you must be willing to do is ask hard questions of yourself and answer them honestly. It is also crucial to work with your spouse to come to agreement in these areas. Whether both parents are working outside the home or not, the application of purposeful, united planning and flexible, joint execution are keys to a successful partnership.

TO WORK OR NOT TO WORK?

The initial question that many mothers struggle with is, "Should I work outside the home?" You may face this question at any point in your marriage and family—as you consider whom to marry, as you become pregnant with your first child, as you consider going back to work after being home full time with children for a while. Some women do not have the luxury of asking that question because working is the only choice they have. If that is your situation, may our heavenly Father richly bless you in it. Hopefully the ideas below will be of help to you in establishing a work–life balance and a loving and happy family.

For those moms who do have a choice about whether to work outside the home, this section will not give you a definitive answer to that question. Rather, here are some key questions for you and your husband. By answering these honestly, realistically, and prayerfully, you should be able to find for yourself the best path for your specific circumstances.

THE MACRO QUESTIONS

First, here is a big-picture question to ask yourself: *What will best enable our family to fulfill our shared family vision?* In other words, considering what we want our family to be in ten, twenty, or thirty years (per the shared family vision we developed in chapter 3), which choice will best help us to fulfill that vision? Once you have established a family vision, use it as a framework to help make important decisions like this one.

Asking yourselves "What path will help us to better fulfill our long-term family vision?" is much different than the questions most moms ask themselves. Questions like, "Do I want to go to work?" "Am I wasting my college degree if I don't work?" "Can we afford to have me stay at home full time?" are usually not the best ways to frame this critical choice. The right question frames the decision in terms of the common goals of the whole family; the wrong questions will focus on self and/ or foolishly isolate one consideration above all others. How you go about deciding whether to get a job outside the home reflects what you value and love most. Is it your own desires and plans, or your family as a team, a unit? The Bible tells us, "A man reaps what he sows" (Gal. 6:7). If you sow selfishness, you will reap the strife that follows from a family of selfish people. So let's start by asking the right question that will prioritize our family and our shared vision for our family's future.

ARE MY HUSBAND AND I
IN AGREEMENT?

Nothing will be more disastrous than to make a decision of this magnitude if you and your husband are not in agreement, especially since the decision you make about your working outside the home will have huge and wide-ranging ramifications on your husband. It will affect how much flexibility your husband will need in his work hours, travel, and career choices. That will in turn impact his career path. If you do not squarely face the reality of what your job situation will mean for your husband, or if he has not agreed to bear those burdens, he will either ignore what's needed from him, or he will bear those burdens with resentment and bitterness, leading to a toxic environment for your marriage.

Many plans to work outside the home result in stress, chaos, and broken marriages because there was no solid ground of agreement and commitment by both husband and wife. One thing that can provide a huge relief for the stresses and strains of work is your husband's constant support. But that is very unlikely to come about unless you talk about it up front and agree to shoulder the burdens together, whatever the decision might be.

That way, if you need to bear down and put in extra hours at your job for a period of time, (hopefully) your husband will pick up the slack and cheer you on. When you get so overwhelmed that you want to cry out, "I just can't do this anymore," your husband assures you of his love and says "It's okay if you want to quit," which of course frees you up to keep going if you want to. You need both oars to be rowing together—don't even try to go it alone.

CHECK YOUR ASSUMPTIONS . . . ARE THEY VALID?

Far too many moms come into important decision-making processes with default assumptions, some or many of which are invalid. We have each gotten some pressure from our mothers, our families, and our friends to buy into one set of assumptions or another, instead of validating these key assumptions for ourselves. For some, it is an assumption that we should pursue our careers exactly as we would have done if we were unmarried or if we had no children. For others, it is an assumption that once we have a family we would stay home full time with the children no matter what. Don't simply accept others' assumptions. You have a wonderful opportunity to proactively create the family life that you and your husband believe will be best for your entire family.

If you have assumed you would work, take the time to think through the benefits (and not just the costs) of perhaps devoting your gifts and talents more directly to your children. What do you see in the families with stay-at-home moms that you admire, that you may want to have in your own family? How could you see your relationship with your children being different if you stayed home? Again, make sure to think through your assumptions carefully, making sure that they are all valid for your family in this season.

If you have assumed you would stay home, take the time to

think through why you are making that assumption. Women today have an extremely wide-ranging spectrum of adsorbed beliefs about work—from the very traditional (men at work, women at home) to old-fashioned feminism (women *must* do exactly what a man can do) to modern feminism (where many are cycling back to traditional assumptions). Be aware of and go beyond your own biases. Make a wise decision that is right for you and your family situation.

What Is the Right Decision for This Season of Our Lives?

What is the right decision for us *today*? Sometimes as we think through these questions we lose sight of a very important fact: life is not static. Your infant will one day go to school, and your child care needs will be different; your husband's income may go up, or he may lose his job; your skills will be in greater demand, or they may become outdated.

In our homes and in the job market, the one constant is change. So, for good or for ill, the decision you make today is not a permanent one—it only needs to be the right one for this season. This reality provides tremendous freedom and comfort as you look at your situation today and make the best decision you can, without feeling trapped. Is it simply unfeasible for you to pursue your career right now? It may not be in a few short years, so enjoy the time you have with your children today! Do you have to work when you would rather be home with your children? That day may come sooner than you think—be faithful to your job and family the best you can be now. So let's hold our decisions lightly, always praying for our heavenly Father's good guidance and great wisdom. Change is constant, but so is His understanding and love.

IMPORTANT MICRO QUESTIONS

Once you have worked through some of these big-picture questions, you can ask the nitty-gritty questions about details that will help you, with your husband, to know what to do for today given who you are, what your family is like, and what your own situation is. The key to making a good decision is being completely realistic and honest with yourself and your spouse. Here are some questions you will want to address:

- What exactly is the net financial benefit of the job? When it comes down to it, most of us (men and women) work primarily for the practical and noble reason of providing for our family and others. If so, then you need to do a hard-nosed accounting of the real costs and benefits of working. You might be surprised to find that an extra sixty thousand dollars in annual income ends up being less than half that after taxes, child care, commuting costs, and all the hidden expenses of work life.

- How would your work demands fit in with your husband's work demands? Are your two jobs compatible? A scenario in which one or both spouses have lower-stress, more-flexible jobs is a completely different scenario than one in which both have demanding, incompatible schedules, whether high paying or not. Be realistic as you assess what that really looks like, and whether it is really doable.

- Are you sure you need that extra income? Life is made up of smaller decisions that inevitably lead to bigger decisions. Reconsider the littler decisions: Do you really need two Starbucks a day (or whatever)? Or larger decisions such as: Do you really need to send your children to that private school instead of the public one or even homeschooling? Do you really need a beach vacation every year instead of going to the park to play? Does that bathroom really need to be remodeled? Sometimes if you take the time to look at a "need" in a different, creative way, you may end up with a different answer.

- Are you satisfied with the child care arrangements you would have if you worked? This is a critical question and one that must be faced directly. For working mothers with younger children, child care is without a doubt one of the highest stress factors. Rather than assuming whatever options there are will be good enough, give careful thought to whether even the best of your available options is good enough. Remember, this is only an issue for a few initial years of a child's life—usually the few years before he or she goes to school. If your child care options are simply not good enough for your comfort, consider delaying the decision to work.

This is not an exhaustive list of questions that should be asked; they are merely illustrative to encourage you to do an honest, realistic assessment. The key is to drill down into the current situation of your own family. Don't forget to ask our heavenly Father for His guidance. He loves the prayers of His people, especially when we are asking for guidance and direction. Above all, please do not shortchange the process and stumble into an answer, relying on cursory impressions and long-held assumptions. Talk at length with your husband, your children, and your closest friends/mentors. Ask hard questions. Be sure your whole family is onboard with whatever decision you make for this season. Be wise. Be honest. Be flexible. Be prayerful.

Mary's Story

My good friend Mary grew up in a classic Asian immigrant family: her parents gave up everything in Korea to move to the United States for a better life for their children. She worked hard through high school and college and fulfilled her parent's dream by attending Harvard Law School. It is an understatement to say that her parents had great expectations for her career. She graduated with honors, took a job in a prestigious law firm in New York City, and moved through several well-planned career steps until she met her wonderful husband in her early thirties. They married and soon after, when she became pregnant, she was confronted with the decision of what to do after the baby was born.

There was pressure from all sides. Her parents said she couldn't "waste" her Harvard education; at the same time, no woman she knew in her church worked after having children. She had always envisioned spending all her time with her baby, but she also had a hard time changing what she had always done: striving for ever-greater achievement. Her husband, thankfully, was absolutely supportive of whatever decision they made.

When they blocked out all the extraneous noise and really thought about it, it came down to this: What would enable them to be the best mother and father they could be to their child?

In her case, it meant she would work part time rather than full time, which, no matter how you look at it, limited her career path. It meant that her husband would have to ask for and maintain flexibility in his job, which also limited his career choices. For them, to be the best mother and father meant logging the extra hours at home, physically being with and interacting daily with their children, and they ordered their work lives to maximize those priorities.

Once that decision was made, Mary was blessed to be offered a great job as a part-time in-house counsel and gained the support of a wonderful boss who valued her contribution enough to keep providing her with flexibility. She has been at this job for fifteen years, while simultaneously homeschooling three children. She often feels uncomfortable juggling three jobs: teacher, lawyer, home manager. But in reality she knows that only one job is the most important: being a mother.

THE WORKING MOM GUIDE

Mary recently read in a blog, "You know you're a working mom when you call time spent commuting back and forth to work 'me time.'"[3] This isn't even really humorous because it's true for so many. Waves of extreme stress have come and gone, but Mary distinctly remembers long stretches of time when she felt like every second of her day needed to be measured, managed, and maximized. Being a mom is universally hard, but being a mom with a job outside the home has some extreme challenges. Even though it is more and more prevalent—in fact, according to the US Census Bureau, about two-thirds of all mothers have jobs outside the home[4]—it is still a hard nut to crack.

How do you become the competent, creative, responsive, go-to problem solver at your job and also be the supportive, loving wife to your husband? Not to mention: feed your family healthy meals; help your children academically; exercise so you can be healthy; be a loving, helpful neighbor; keep up with your best friend from high school; get the kids to their games, practices, and doctor's appointments . . . the list goes on and on.

Here is the biggest secret that all working moms learn: *you can't do it all!* Trying to be the perfect employee, wife, friend, and mother is an exhausting chase after a figment of our cultural imagination. This chase will only lead to frustration, guilt, burnout, and misery for your entire family. Close your ears to the siren song of perfection. Accept your limitations and your right to say, "I just can't do that." It is okay. Not even Jesus did everything when He was on earth.

Pursuing Excellence, Not Success

The primary guiding principle that has given Mary meaning and wholeness at work has been the pursuit of excellence. She quickly saw that she could not stress out about promotions, recognition, raises, or any other external goal. These could not be her primary goals but by-products. Her advice to herself has been what we tell our kids all the time: simply and always do your best. This applies to anyone who has a job.

Tackle all your tasks and projects with integrity, faithfulness, and servant-mindedness. The Bible tells us this is the right approach for many reasons. Doing the right thing the right way is its own reward. Sometimes it is even recognized!

But external rewards cannot be the end goal. Our job is to do the very best we can. In Mary's case, pursuing excellence and not results has paid huge dividends in her ability to balance work and home.

There are other benefits to this approach. A boss who has an excellent worker is generally going to go out of her way for that employee. Is your child suddenly sick and you have to leave early or work from home? A boss that values you will make that work. Do you want to make a commitment to be home with your family for dinner each night? You need to become such a trusted, valued employee that the boss will wholeheartedly say, "I don't care how the work gets done, as long as it keeps getting done well." It is shocking how rare it is to find employees who are sincerely committed to excellence and true service. When bosses see this kind of dedication, it usually does not go unnoticed. This is a golden ticket to relieving the stress of balancing work and family. Show by your excellence day in and day out that you can be trusted to do great work in all situations. Help them realize that they don't want to lose you and over time you will win yourself much needed flexibility.

Another natural result of pursuing excellence at work is advancement in your job. Once again, this should not be a primary goal, but it naturally becomes a by-product of your commitment to excellence. Promotions can provide you with more flexibility in balancing work and life. It does not mean less work, since usually more will be demanded of you as you advance. However, in many fields career advancement means you have more control over your schedule, which can greatly relieve the stress of managing your time.

Often the stress of work is not so much in the amount or

intensity of the work itself; rather, it's when you need to be at a parent-teacher conference and someone schedules a meeting right in that time slot. So the key is often gaining a better ability to manage both worlds. Simply put, the higher your position, the more you can make things happen, rather than having them happen to you. Rather than having to ask the shift manager whether you can have certain days or times off, you will be the shift manager setting the shifts. Rather than having to put in "face time" at work, you will be the boss who makes it clear no one needs to stay late just to have face time. The best bargaining chip you will bring to negotiating with your boss will not be a plea for sympathy. It will be that you are an excellent and valued employee, one who can command the flexibility you need.

MODELING A SOLID WORK ETHIC

One of the best gifts we can give to our children is modeling a solid work ethic. You help them build a foundation for success when you model working hard and cheerfully, intent on adding value to whatever you do. Albert Einstein famously said, "Strive not to be a success, but rather to be of value." These kinds of values are not only taught, but in the most meaningful way they are caught. There is a less solid work ethic these days, and we will be doing a great service to society to raise children who have a solid one. A job well done is it own reward, and we want to model this ethos to our children.

Finally, it is vitally important for our children to see that, while we are sincere and hardworking, our jobs are not the most important thing in our lives. Children need to see and know that the Lord and our families are the two most important things in the world. It is a tremendous gift for our children to experience this reality firsthand. It will provide a road map for them to follow as they grow up and raise families of their own. It will especially provide a valuable compass not only for our daughters, who are looking for guidance on how to think about their futures including work and family, but also for our sons who will need to know what a compatible view of work and family should be. Just think, you are building not only a healthy family for yourself, but a legacy of healthy families for generations to come as you model excellence at work in the context of unwavering commitment to your family.

FLEXIBILITY AND PRAYER ARE KEY

The value of flexibility in a mom's job allows the needs of home to be handled. A sick child, the child care provider being suddenly unavailable, the call from the principal's office—these can be tremendously stressful if there is no ability to deal with them during your working schedule. The flexibility you have earned through your excellent work will help to relieve these stresses. The other side of the coin is your flexibility to handle the emergencies of work. In many jobs there will be ebbs and flows of demands: an extra shift that needs to be covered for a coworker, a public relations disaster that explodes unexpectedly, tax season for accountants. If you are completely unavailable to help absorb these hits, it will be difficult to ask for flexibility from your boss when you need it.

This kind of porosity between job and family is not easy to manage. It can easily become unbalanced. It takes concerted effort to exercise wisdom in one's circumstance and a commitment to integrity, but striving for wholeness between work and family is well worth the effort. But be warned, it does take effort. Each time someone at work calls you because "it's an emergency," you will need to handle it with discernment and muster up all the grace and charm you can. When it truly is urgent and you are really needed, you will need to make the extra effort to manage your family and home around the crisis. When it is not truly urgent, you will need all your wits about you to talk your boss or colleague off the ledge in a way that makes clear your commitment to the company. Is this easy to do? No way! Will you blow it from time to time? Yes, certainly. But as you practice this balance over time trust is built. Over time, that trust will pay huge dividends in reducing the tug of war between work and home.

It is also essential that working moms learn to do what the apostle Paul encourages us to do daily: to "pray continually" (1 Thess. 5:17). You will be amazed at some of the answers our heavenly Father will send you. He understands better than anyone else the dual challenges you face. If you take time to ask Him for His help, He will take time to help you, sometimes in amazing ways.

The primary guiding principle that has given Mary wholeness at home has been aiming for love instead of performance. She freely admits that she at times fails at this. We women are extremely hard on ourselves and sometimes our children, often setting impossible standards for everyone. This pursuit of performance is an insidious weed that has to be consciously, daily uprooted so that the beautiful flowers of love and grace can grow in its place. How do we do this? Mary has found certain disciplines essential for the working mom. The first is embracing the spiritual discipline of humility.

THE IMPORTANCE OF HUMILITY

We need to be a careful student of ourselves, of our abilities and limits. Some people are natural dynamos of energy; they appear to have enormous reserves of physical energy, emotional energy, relational energy, and intellectual energy. They seem capable of staying physically fit (they jog five miles every day at five o'clock in the morning), keeping up with their mother and best friends (they talk almost every day), reading interesting books and being able to talk about them charmingly at dinner parties. They can also listen sympathetically to their preteens emote about stuff while making a fabulous dinner for the family. Realistically, we see one woman who does some of those things and another woman who does others, and we feel compelled to do it all. But that is not reality.

All of us moms, whether working outside the home or not, must recognize our limitations. This is difficult because it means we must be willing to embrace our finiteness, in reality to embrace humility. This is absolutely necessary. Here is what happens if we don't embrace humility: we try to do it all, keeping up a mad pace until our children or other people get in the way. Then we become frustrated and angry; we feel like failures, easily leading into depression. The world becomes a miserable place, not only for the mom but for everyone around her. As they say "If Mama ain't happy, ain't nobody happy."

Experience, however, is a wonderful teacher. Over time, Mary has learned that for there to be peace and joy in her family, she has to humbly accept her limitations. She can have a nice home-cooked family dinner for the kids' birthdays, but perhaps it is best if she doesn't organize a super-fun slumber party for ten of her son's closest friends. She can try to see her childhood best friends when she flies out to see her parents, but joining in a girls' weekend getaway is not possible at this point in her life. Life for moms is a matter of prioritizing. Mary is at peace knowing that her first priority is to be a mother whose children know without a doubt that she loves and treasures them, even if that means other priorities might take a hit.

Recognizing our limitations helps us see what we can't do so that we don't wear ourselves and others out by impossible standards. It also helps us appreciate what we can do so that we can make the most of what God has given to each of us. It brings wholeness and peace, a wonderful gift we can give to our children.

THE BLESSING OF MARGIN

A related discipline Mary has learned as a working mom is the importance of leaving margin in our lives. Mary values efficiency; she wants every minute to lead to some accomplishment. The fact that working mothers have so little spare time feeds this frenzy and makes us especially vulnerable to margin creep. As we try to squeeze out any fluff, we end up squeezing out any margin in our lives and the lives of our children. Mary did not realize early enough how much stress this piled on her and her family. In addition to being a working mom, Mary homeschools her kids. As she progressed in both areas, she realized that she was losing her patience with her kids because she did not embrace margin in her life.

For a number of years her children spent the morning in homeschool with Mary, then she would drop them off with grandparents for the afternoon while she went to work. At lunchtime after she had squeezed in the maximum amount of instruction, she would change frantically from sweatpants into a suit and jacket. As she shoveled in lunch she barked orders to the kids that "it's time to go." They had such trouble with shoes! Her heart would be pounding with impatience and frustration as her eight-year-old could find only one shoe, her six-year-old was taking forever to tie his, and she had to wrestle the three-year-old into his. She still cringes at how she yelled at them because they couldn't tie their shoes fast enough. They would cry. Mary would cry and feel absolutely wretched. Every day wasn't like this, but there were enough of these days that she finally realized something had to change.

As a Chinese proverb says, "The best time to plant a tree was twenty years ago. The second best time is now." Mary realized that a tremendously helpful asset for working moms and their children is simply to build in some margin. Leave a cushion because little people (and big people) are not perfect and can't keep to a perfect schedule. If you need to be somewhere at 1:00 p.m., plan to be there at 12:50. If you think it will take ten minutes to get everyone's coat and shoes on, plan for fifteen minutes. Simply leaving room for the unexpected will allow you to be gracious when mistakes are made and to be calm when the unexpected happens.

This little thing has made such a difference in Mary's family. She still struggles with trying to fit too much in. But when she starts to feel the tension rise, one of the first things she looks for is whether she has forgotten the margin. Fixing that problem usually results in an immediate change to the family happiness quotient. Be encouraged: your gentleness and kindness will be tremendous blessings for your children and will bring wholeness to you too.

ACCEPTING OUR CHILDREN FOR WHO THEY REALLY ARE

We moms must also choose to accept our children for who they are and not according to our hopes or expectations. This is a universal issue for all mothers, but it can be especially challenging for working moms. In the limited time working mothers have, it is easier to assess performance of children according to some set parameters than to know and accept them in all their lumpiness.

The worst day of Mary's parenting life was the day she got so stressed and angry that she screamed at her children and abandoned them to retreat to her room. Mary's eleven-year-old son wrote this letter and slid it under the door:

> Dear Mama,
>   We still love you. We don't at all hate you. So don't act like we do. Please don't act like we should be perfect. If we were, we wouldn't be human. Or, for that matter, your children. So, please, if you aren't still angry, please come to the schoolroom and we can talk this over. But if you hate us we will stay in our rooms till Papa comes. And we will know you don't love us. We hope you don't love a camera, or a kitchen, or perfection, more than your children. But it's getting hard to tell.

Mary's eleven-year-old signed it and her six-year-old printed his name (Mary's nine-year-old daughter, probably feeling it was disloyal, did not). The saving grace is that children are so incredibly forgiving and so desirous of a warm relationship with their mom that reconciliation came quickly. All was forgiven and forgotten by Mary's children. Mary keeps that letter in her purse to remind herself what she must avoid: being so caught up in goals and plans that she causes her children to think, for even one moment, that she loves anything more than them. Building in sufficient daily margin helps her avoid that trap.

Mary still struggles with her tendency to focus on whether her kids got their homework done, how they are doing in school, how their piano or violin playing is coming, and so on. But when she takes the time to let them talk about inconsequential things, when she listens to them act out a scene with their stuffed animals, when she takes her teenagers to the movies, it reassures them that she loves them simply for who they are. In the end, the greatest gift we can give to our children is the knowledge that we see them, we know them, and we love them for who they are and not what we want them to be. By including God in our endeavors and lifting it back to Him, a job outside the home can be managed to underscore (and not overwhelm) the love we have for our children. That isn't easy, but by asking the tough questions, being sure that the whole family is onboard, humbly accepting our limitations, staying flexible, and creating needed margin (among other things) it can be done.

Ponder

God's Word

Therefore, as God's chosen people, holy and dearly loved, clothe yourselves with compassion, kindness, humility, gentleness and patience. . . . Let the peace of Christ rule in your hearts. . . . And whatever you do, whether in word or deed, do it all in the name of the Lord Jesus, giving thanks to God the Father through him. (Col. 3:12, 15, 17)

The fruit of the Spirit is love, joy, peace, forbearance, kindness, goodness, faithfulness, gentleness and self-control. (Gal. 5:22–23)

Whatever you do, work at it with all your heart, as working for the Lord, not for human masters. (Col. 3:23)

The Authors' Words

"Simply leaving room for the unexpected will allow you to be gracious when mistakes are made and to be calm when the unexpected happens."

Assess

1. Why is excellence the goal instead of success?
2. How can you aim for excellence but still humbly accept your limitations?
3. Do you build enough margin into your daily plans? What hindrances do you face?

4. Whether you work outside the home or not, what are the most important truths to communicate to your children?
5. What lessons have you learned through this chapter?

Sum Up

Modern families have to wisely make choices; this is both liberating and daunting. But whatever works best for your family, refuse to listen to the siren song of perfection. Once you do, you can be free to joyfully and courageously pursue your vision for your family.

Thirteen

Dynamic Moms:
A Spirit-Led Ministry

Linda is the mother of a handicapped child. Both she and her husband, Rob, were shattered by the diagnosis of cerebral palsy of their much-anticipated little boy. They had none of the genetic markers that would have indicated possible health issues for their unborn child. In the Asian culture in which they had been raised, being handicapped is not only perceived as a family tragedy, but it is often viewed as a curse. Ashamed, many Asian families hide the problem and the disabled child remains a family secret.

For several years Linda remained isolated with her child, depressed and almost invisible. Linda read many books on parenting handicapped kids, and she scoured the Internet for information. After several years, brought to the end of her strength, she and her husband finally came to the realization that they did not have the wisdom or the power to deal with the situation. While they were in a position to financially provide for their much-loved son, there was nothing they could do to fundamentally alter the situation.

Statistically, they knew that a majority of all couples with severely handicapped kids divorce due to the overwhelming stress and sadness of daily life. She and her husband were not interested in the Christian faith until they encountered a situation that only put fear and dread in their hearts. Through friends, they started attending their local church. They came to realize it would only be through God's ministry to them and their family that they would have hope of surviving their brokenness. This family tragedy has become a testimony of God's grace and power. Linda and Rob would never have chosen this path to know God, but they now have a deep faith and a quiet peace that has enabled them to build a stronger marriage and a happier family than they ever thought possible.

GOD'S STRENGTH IN OUR WEAKNESS

Linda and Rob often share their favorite scripture in the Bible: "'My grace is sufficient for you, for my power is made perfect in weakness.' Therefore I will boast all the more gladly about my weaknesses, so that Christ's power may rest on me" (2 Cor. 12:9). God brought strength and power into Linda's family through what the world perceives as weakness. The Lord often uses a paradox to teach us His deepest truths: by being weak, Linda and her husband became strong. When we are humbled, God can truly minister to us. We in turn can minister to our families through His power.

Mothering is ultimately about being a minister of God's grace to our families, and we can only do this if we embrace our weakness and look to His power. Our ministry in the family is of truly great importance to the Lord. He knows we need His dynamic power. If we ask Him, He will not hold back. Moms are God's ministers to families, and we are empowered by the Holy Spirit to accomplish His will on earth. We don't live humdrum lives of no importance; we lead lives of eternal significance. What we do will reverberate down through the generations and impact our world for generations to come. The power of the Holy Spirit enables us to put our faith into practical action. Though being a mom is immensely practical, moms are also spiritual ministers. The Lord has graciously made His Holy Spirit available to all believers so that we can be empowered:

> And it shall come to pass afterward
> That I will pour out My Spirit on all flesh;
> Your sons and your daughters shall prophesy,
> Your old men shall dream dreams,
> Your young men shall see visions. (Joel 2:28 NKJV)

I am humbled when I look back at my mothering. I see all the things I could have done better. But the great news is that Jesus does not see my mothering through the prism of judgment. He knows my human frailty, and He created me to be an overcomer. He has created all of us with the need to experience daily renewal in our lives and families. His Spirit is the answer to our brokenness and our deepest needs. His power is available to all who believe. Wholeness, healing, and health are available to all those who are connected to Jesus.

Renewing, dynamic power comes from the Holy Spirit. We all need the daily empowerment of the Holy Spirit in the face of the demands and challenges that come our way. The Spirit pro-vides that touch of encouragement we need in a long day. When my own spirit is wilting because I have been up nights with sick kids, or am facing a week alone because Gregory is away on a business trip, the Holy Spirit has ministered to my deepest needs.

THE POWER OF GOD'S HOLY SPIRIT

We are all born with a deep hunger for His Spirit. We were cre-ated by God to require His power in order to accomplish His will on earth and in our families. In fact, we can do nothing eternal without His power. We will all pass on from these mortal bodies, and it will only be His glory that remains. If I want to be a part of His kingdom on earth, if I want my children to be wise adults in a foolish generation, then I need to be in the Spirit, and the Spirit must indwell me.

The word *power* is used 120 times in the New Testament, so there is much to learn on the subject. Spiritual power is the ability to move God's kingdom forward on earth and in our families. The words *power* and *dynamic* share the same root in the Greek language. God's power gives me, and every mom, the dynamism we require in the raising of our kids.

During Jesus' ministry in Israel, He said it was a good thing that He was leaving because "unless I go away, the Advocate [Holy Spirit] will not come to you" (John 16:7). Jesus was not afraid to leave His disciples because He knew that they would be getting even greater power to accomplish His purpose on earth. The early church was getting a blast of dynamic power that would change the course of history. This same power is what changes the course of our families. Jesus told His disciples that they "will receive power when the Holy Spirit comes on you" (Acts 1:8). Not only does the power of God enable us to effectively serve our family, but the Holy Spirit reveals our family's deepest needs and helps us set the right goals. Jesus said that the Holy Spirit will guide us into all truth (John 16:13). Young families need the Spirit to give them guidance and wisdom. Families well along the way need a continuous infusion of joy and constancy. We all need the fruit of the Spirit that the Bible promises: "love, joy, peace, forbearance, kindness, goodness, faithfulness, gentleness and self-control" (Gal. 5:22–23).

The Holy Spirit's purpose is to create in us fullness and joy. The Holy Spirit wants to empower us in the face of temptations and brokenness. This is good news for the weary mom: God gives us the power of the Spirit in order to live, and to live abundantly. As Jesus told us, "I have come that they may have life, and that they may have it more abundantly" (John 10:10 NKJV). We need His power to help us live at a level we could not achieve on our own. We need to meditate on this promise: "For God has not given us a spirit of fear, but of power and of love and of a sound mind" (2 Tim. 1:7 NKJV).

The dynamic power of the Holy Spirit is what has freed me from the pervasive brokenness of my own childhood. I may have been broken by events in my mother's womb and in my childhood, but over the years He has been able to accomplish in me His purposes of peace and wholeness. My husband and I, by His grace and mercy, have not replicated our pasts in our own family. Through prayerful study of the Scriptures and the Holy Spirit's power, we have developed a family vision that makes our family our priority. Through the power of the Spirit, we are coming to see that vision take shape.

It is not the end goal that is complicated; it is the fact that the daily working out of our faith is foreign to our human nature. Only by allowing the Holy Spirit to work in our lives can we develop the self-discipline required to daily take up the cross and walk in belief. Through the Holy Spirit's work over time our Father's desires become our desires. Through the Spirit we are changed to be more like Jesus. As John the Baptist proclaimed, "He must increase, but I must decrease" (John 3:30 NKJV). In a world of wounded souls, the answer is the increase of the Spirit in our lives. I bear witness to His redeeming power. The Holy Spirit works in our lives to heal us and make us pleasing to the Father. He helps us grow in the character of Jesus as evidenced by the fruit of the Spirit in our lives. That is the help I need every day to be a better mother, wife, and person.

We all need to draw on God's dynamic power continually as we develop the essential ingredients for our mothering. Without His power we will eventually grow weary and discouraged. It is all too easy in the tyranny of the trivial to put time with God last in our overly busy schedules. But it is His daily nurturing that we most need to be moms who raise our children well. It is the well of "living water" from which we must draw our sustenance (John 7:38).

The Spirit of Truth and Humility

The Spirit helps us as followers of Christ by filling us with His truth. As Jesus promised us in John 16:13: "When he, the Spirit of truth, comes, he will guide you into all the truth." Truth is vital to any family; it is akin to the mortar that holds bricks together. It is not always seen, and it is easy to skimp on. But it is always needed, and when it is not used properly, the entire structure is at risk. This is where the Holy Spirit can help you if you ask for His help. Ask Him to make you aware of any deviations from the truth that might be hurting your family. It is rather common for our teenagers and young adults to tell little fibs (or outright lies) when telling the truth would be difficult. But the Holy Spirit knows what is true and what is not. If you sincerely ask the Spirit to reveal the truth to you about your children, He will. Let me add, however, that you must be in listening mode and you must be willing to hear what He is saying.

Both my husband and I have relatives who are habitual liars. It has brought devastation to them and to others. Satan is known in the Bible as the "father of lies" (John 8:44). We never want our kids to take on satanic characteristics. That is why all parents have to raise their kids to value the truth and to be truth tellers. By esteeming truth, we draw closer to God and to freedom because Jesus promises us that "the truth will set you free" (John 8:32).

One of the most inspiring character traits of the Holy Spirit is His humility. He enters our lives at our conversion in order to draw us to Jesus. The Holy Spirit does not draw attention to Himself. He does not glorify Himself; He glorifies Jesus. In this same way we are not to work for our own glory, but to walk in humility and glorify the Lord. If we do not humbly acknowledge our need for the Holy Spirit, we will be greatly hampered in our lives. One of the deepest lessons I have learned about motherhood is that it is a humbling endeavor. I have come to recognize how very much I need the Holy Spirit so that I can be the best mom I can be.

If we are not humble, we will look to ourselves and to earthly solutions that may work in the short term but rarely solve the underlying issues. He empowers us, but only if we allow Him to work in our lives. The Holy Spirit does not force us to look to Him, nor does He force us to obey Him. When we humbly acknowledge our need, He will be released to work through us, our lives, and our circumstances. The Holy Spirit will create the dynamic we need in our lives. It is the work of the Spirit to combat the spirits of our age, including turmoil, strife, and selfishness, and replace them with the peace, love, and joy of the Lord.

THE DYNAMIC POWER OF HEARTFELT PRAYER

Like many parents, Mrs. Taylor was perplexed by what her young adult son wanted to do with his life. Hudson had been a frail child, and she and her husband were concerned about his future. As he neared the age of twenty, he launched into a bookkeeping career. Hudson had some faith, but it was more of an afterthought. Since he still lived with his parents, Hudson begrudgingly sat down to family devotions and attended church. His eyes glazed over during the Bible readings and church sermons. Hudson felt spiritual instruction held little relevance for his life.

Mrs. Taylor resolved to pray for her son every day. One afternoon, while Mrs. Taylor was visiting her sister for a few weeks, she felt a strong urging from the Holy Spirit to spend hours praying earnestly for her son. That same afternoon Hudson found several spiritual tracts at home and from reading these tracts he felt impelled to give his life to Jesus. Hudson Taylor went on to found China Inland Mission; this ministry was mightily used by God to bring the gospel to China. Today, China has more than one hundred million Christians, due in part to the powerful ministry of Hudson Taylor. His ministry can be wonderfully traced back to the dynamic prayers of his mother. My own husband was brought to Christ through a Chinese family who had come to know the Lord in the nineteenth century through China Inland Mission. The Slayton family is very grateful to Mrs. Taylor and her prayers.

Our Father releases His Spirit into our prayer lives if we humbly ask Him. This can make our prayers the most powerful and effective weapon that we have as mothers. "The prayer of a righteous person is powerful and effective," the Bible tells us in James 5:16. But it is impossible for any of us to be righteous without the atoning work of Christ and the covering of His Spirit. That is where the power comes from; it does not come from within ourselves.

Since my debilitating illness commenced two years ago, our children pray for me daily. They are asking for the complete healing of my facial paralysis and the exhaustion I daily battle. My nineteen-year-old said he believed that God would do something "big" through my illness. It will be only through the power of the Holy Spirit that I will be healed, since my doctors are unanimous that the damage is irreversible. But already I have gone further in my healing than the doctors foretold; I was told I would not be able to smile naturally and now I can. And my husband's and children's prayers have released me from fear and depression. Humbly acknowledging our need for God's Holy Spirit through prayer can transform any family, any situation.

MAKING YOUR HOUSE A "HOUSE OF PRAYER"

God called His house "a house of prayer" (Matt. 21:13). When we pray, we intercede for our families. Every day I pray with

Gregory for our children. When our children call from wherever they are in the world, we pray together before we hang up the phone. We pray before every meal and before our most difficult discussions. Our youngest prays with us both at the start of the day and at its end. Prayer draws us together, and it draws us closer to the Lord. We grow in our knowledge of who God is and what He desires. There is nothing that bonds us more than when we are in prayer. It is wonderful to contemplate that while we are praying, Jesus Himself is seated at the right hand of the Father making intercession for us, and the Holy Spirit is at work to answer those prayers.

As children, in order to learn to speak, we must first learn to listen. This is absolutely essential in our relationship with the Lord: "Be still, and know that I am God" (Ps. 46:10). Listening is vital. We are changed by being in the presence of God. In listening to our God, over time we are transformed. Effective listening is as important with our children as it is with the Lord. Through our listening, our kids will reveal who they are. Listening will help us understand how they are evolving and who they are becoming. Through listening to God, we will evolve and become the moms the Lord wants us to be.

Listening to what God is saying is essential in our prayer life. We have to stop talking in prayer and start listening. It is in prayer and worship that we humble ourselves before God. We are helpless without His power. Our prayers exhibit faith that He is able to answer our supplications. It is in that humble relationship with God that His power is unleashed.

Listening prayer is my spiritual lifeline to the Lord. It has given God an opening into my life even when I feel far from Him. It can be a lifeline into your lives and the lives of your children if you cultivate this spiritual discipline. Prayer is a major component to every dynamic mothering ministry. Prayer is one sure way we can tap into God's dynamic power for our lives via the Holy Spirit.

From the womb, pray for your child and continue to pray every day. Ultimately, it will be our children's decision to choose to follow Christ, but as we keep releasing the Spirit into their lives through prayer, we can trust God to move on their behalf. Moms and children need to pray together and commit our daily activities to Jesus. Spirit-filled prayer changes everyone.

God is utterly committed to our children's welfare, for they are His children too. No matter how deep our love is for our children, Jesus loves them even more than we do. In Isaiah 54:13 He promises that:

> all your children will be taught by the LORD,
> and great will be their peace.

We can see from this promise that He Himself is on the journey of motherhood with us. He is more than able to raise whole children in a broken generation such as ours. Jesus loves us, guides us, and blesses us so that we in turn are able to love, guide, and bless our family in His glorious Name. God promised us this: "Not by might nor by power, but by my Spirit" (Zech. 4:6). Through His Spirit, by faith and prayer over time, we can become the spiritually dynamic moms He has always meant us to be.

Ponder

God's Word

You will receive power when the Holy Spirit comes on you. (Acts 1:8)

When he, the Spirit of truth, comes, he will guide you into all the truth. (John 16:13)

And it shall come to pass afterward
That I will pour out My Spirit on all flesh;
Your sons and your daughters shall prophesy,
Your old men shall dream dreams,
Your young men shall see visions. (Joel 2:28 NKJV)

The prayer of a righteous person is powerful and effective. (James 5:16)

The Authors' Words

"We all need to draw on God's dynamic power continually as we develop the essential ingredients for our mothering. Without His power we will eventually grow weary and discouraged."

Assess

1. How does the Holy Spirit personally minister to you?
2. Are you looking to the Holy Spirit to empower your children and knit your family together? Are you confident that this is God's will?

3. Are you listening to God? How do you hear Him?
4. The ministry of prayer is a powerful one; how can you make your own house a "house of prayer"? What will you commit to prayer every day?
5. Are you trusting the Lord for your children's future? Do you trust the Lord to accomplish His will in the lives of your children?

Sum Up

Mothers are God's ministers to our families. God empowers us, through the Holy Spirit, to do His will—and what we do will reverberate down through the generations. Always remember that as a mom, your ministry to your family has eternal significance. Make it count!

Acknowledgments

This book began with much support, and I warmly thank Ingrid Hill, Jennifer Keisling, and Lisa Wen for all their love and encouragement. I could not have written this book without all your hard work. I admire your mothering and your dedication to faith and family. You have been tremendous examples of what is possible.

Christian Slayton, Ali Mazzara, John Murphy, Michael Tree, and all the members of the Board of the Fellowship of Fathers Foundation have strongly supported our work through prayer, practical efforts, and friendship . . . along with many other dear friends. Thank you and again, thank you.

Many thanks and much appreciation to the wonderful and supportive efforts of our great team at Thomas Nelson.

Blessings on my hardworking, loving husband, without whom there would be no book and even more importantly, no wonderful family and life. And our children, Sasha, Christian, Daniel, and Nicholas. You are all the tangible evidence of God's love in my life.

Notes

Introduction

1. Gregory W. Slayton, *Be a Better Dad Today: Ten Tools Every Father Needs* (Ventura, CA: Regal, 2012).

Chapter 3: The Importance of Vision: Thriving Families

1. David M. Cutler, Edward L. Glaeser, and Karen E. Norberg, "Explaining the Rise in Youth Suicide," National Bureau of Economic Research (2001), http://www.nber.org/chapters/c10690.pdf.

Chapter 4: Breaking Generational Curses: Wholeness Is Possible

1. Jeffrey Kluger, *The Sibling Effect: What the Bonds Among Brothers and Sisters Reveal About Us* (New York: Riverhead, 2011).

Chapter 5: Moms Are Not Perfect: That Never Was the Goal

1. Lorie Johnson, "Shocker! Anti-Depressant Use Up 400 Percent," Christian Broadcasting Network, Healthy Living (blog), September 26, 2012, http://blogs.cbn.com/healthyliving/archive/2012/09/26/shocker-anti-depressant-use-up-400.aspx.

2. Ann Crittenden, *The Price of Motherhood: Why the Most Important Job in the World Is Still the Least Valued* (New York: Metropolitan, 2001).
3. Anne-Marie Slaughter, "Why Women Still Can't Have It All," *The Atlantic,* July/August 2012, http://www.theatlantic.com/magazine /archive/2012/07/why-women-still-cant-have-it-all/309020.
4. Ibid.

Chapter 6: Harvard Versus Heaven: Start with Eternity in Mind

1. Po Bronson, *The Nudist on the Late Shift* (New York: Random House, 1999).
2. Tyler Kingkade, "How Students with Mental Illness Can Prepare for College," The Huffington Post, March 26, 2014, http:// www.huffingtonpost.com/2014/03/26/mental-illness-college -preparing_n_5038181.html.
3. Ibid.
4. Ibid.
5. Ibid.

Chapter 7: Sex, Drugs, and Rock and Roll: Answering Tough Questions

1. Tyler Charles, "(Almost) Everyone's Doing It: A surprising new study shows Christians are having premarital sex and abortions as much (or more) than non-Christians," *Relevant,* September /October 2011, http://www.relevantmagazine.com/life/relationships /almost-everyones-doing-it.
2. Haley Blum, "'Girls' Producers Defend Lena Dunham's Nudity," *USA Today,* January 10, 2014, http:// www.usatoday.com/story/life/people/2014/01/10 /girls-producers-defend-lena-dunhams-nudity/4410633.
3. "Prescription Drug Overdose in the United States: Fact Sheet," Centers for Disease Control and Prevention, http://www.cdc.gov /homeandrecreationalsafety/overdose/facts.html.

Chapter 9: The Three Cs of Motherhood: Communication, Collective Wisdom, and Community

1. John T. Cacioppo and William Patrick, *Loneliness: Human Nature and the Need for Social Connection* (New York: Norton, 2009).
2. Joanna Stern, "Cellphone Users Check Phones 150x/Day and Other Internet Fun Facts," ABC News, Technology Review (blog), May 29, 2013, http://abcnews.go.com/blogs/technology/2013/05 /cellphone-users-check-phones-150xday-and-other-internet-fun-facts.

3. Bryan C. Auday, PhD and Sybil W. Coleman, MSW., MEd., "Pulling Off the Mask: The Impact of Social Networking Activities on Evangelical Christian College Students," Gordon College (Self-Reported Study), August 2009, http://www.gordon.edu/download/pages/Pulling%20 Off%20the%20Mask-Facebook%20Study1.pdf.

Chapter 10: Parenting in the Age of Busy: Time Is Our Friend

1. Kim Brooks, "The Day I Left My Son in the Car," Salon .com, June 3, 2014, http://www.salon.com/2014/06/03 /the_day_i_left_my_son_in_the_car/.
2. Ken Eisold, "Suicide, Loneliness, and the Vulnerability of Men," *Psychology Today*, May 24, 2013, http://www .psychologytoday.com/blog/hidden-motives/201305 /suicide-loneliness-and-the-vulnerability-men.

Chapter 11: Wisdom for Single Moms: Hope Is Available

1. Jonathan Vespa, Jamie M. Lewis, and Rose M. Kreider, "America's Families and Living Arrangements: 2012," Economics and Statistics Administration, http://www.census.gov/prod/2013pubs/p20-570.pdf.
2. Gregory W. Slayton, *Be a Better Dad Today: Ten Tools Every Father Needs* (Ventura, CA: Regal, 2012).

Chapter 12: Working Moms: Excellence, Not Success

1. Sheryl Sandberg and Nell Scovell, *Lean In: Women, Work, and the Will to Lead* (New York: Alfred A. Knopf, 2013).
2. Rosa Brooks, "Recline, Don't 'Lean In' (Why I Hate Sheryl Sandberg)," *Washington Post*, February 25, 2014, http://www .washingtonpost.com/blogs/she-the-people/wp/2014/02/25 /recline-dont-lean-in-why-i-hate-sheryl-sandberg/.
3. Katherine Lewis, "Readers Respond: You Know You're a Working Mom When . . . ," About.com, http://workingmoms.about.com/u/ua /todaysworkingmoms/WorkingMomMadlibs.htm.
4. D'vera Cohn, Gretchen Livingston, and Wendy Wang, "After Decades of Decline, a Rise in Stay-at-Home Mothers," Pew Research Centers Social Demographic Trends Project, http://www.pewsocialtrends.org/2014/04/08 /after-decades-of-decline-a-rise-in-stay-at-home-mothers.

About the Authors

Marina Slayton graduated from Amherst College and completed dual master's degrees at Columbia University. Before she became a mom, she taught at various universities and was the director of a number of adult literacy programs in New England. She was appointed to the Massachusetts Task Force on the Working Poor by Governor Dukakis. She was editor-in-chief of the Bermuda bestseller *Four Centuries of Friendship: US/Bermuda Relations 1609 to 2009* (FourCenturiesOfFriendship.com).

Gregory Slayton graduated with honors from Dartmouth College and Harvard Business School and earned a master's degree in Asian Studies as a US Fulbright Scholar. He has been a Silicon Valley CEO and venture capitalist, a senior US diplomat, and a distinguished visiting professor or lecturer at Harvard, Stanford, and Dartmouth in the USA and UIBE, Szechuan University, and Peking University in China. He coauthored the

Bermuda bestseller *Four Centuries of Friendship: US/Bermuda Relations 1609 to 2009* (FourCenturiesOfFriendship.com). He is also the best-selling author of *Be a Better Dad Today: Ten Tools Every Father Needs* (BeABetterDadToday.com), which has sold over 150,000 copies worldwide. The Slaytons are donating all royalties of the book to pro-family charities throughout the world, including the Fellowship of Fathers Foundation (FellowshipofFathersFoundation.org).

The Slaytons have been married for more than twenty-five years and have four wonderful children, ages fourteen to twenty-five. They divide their time between Greater China and North America.

For more on this book, please visit BeTheBestMomYouCanBe .com. Please join us for interesting conversation on motherhood and fatherhood at Facebook.com/BetheBestMomYouCanBe.

Gregory is also discussing these issues at Facebook.com/ BeaBetterDadToday.

Index

Relevant magazine, 101
religion, of parents, xvi–xvii
repentance, 133
respect, and valuing sex, 108
Resveratrol, 111
rewards, 199–201
rock and roll culture, 115–118
romantic love, 106

S

sacrificial love, 6
Salon.com, 159
Samaritan woman at the well, 162
Sandberg, Sheryl, 189
Sartre, Jean-Paul, 150–151
satanism, 119–120
schools
  choices, 89–93
  drugs in, 113–114
search, for love, 3
security, 19
self-centeredness, 7, 20
self-worth, 82
selfish tendencies, 6–9
sex, 106–109
shopping, as sport, 75
The Sibling Effect (Kluger), 48
sibling rivalry, 48–49
silence, over drug issue, 113–114
sin, recognition of, 46
single moms, 25, 175–188
  counseling for, 182–184
  getting ex-husband involved in
    parenting, 185–186
  learning new parenting methods,
    184–185
Slaughter, Anne-Marie, 71
social media, 147–148
spiritual beauty, 63

standards, 64
stay-at-home moms, devaluation, 70
stress, 205
  in morning, 73
  of work, 200–201
students, mental health of, 95–96
success, xiv, 61
  vs. excellence, 199–201
  measurements of, 64, 84
suffering, 51, 55–57
suicide, 10, 32–33, 67
supernatural, 119
support, 142

T

Taylor, Hudson, 218
teenagers
  communication, 144
  raising, 121–122
  suicides, 32–33
Ten Commandments, 122
thanks, 73–76
Thanksgiving, 146
three Cs, 121
"tiger mom" approach, 88–89
time, for lifelong friendships,
  169–171
tolerance, 104, 108
Tolstoy, Leo, *Anna Karenina*, 2
transformation, and God's power, 51
trivial, tyranny of, 160–163
trust, 53, 86, 203
truth, spirit of, 216–218
TV shows, appropriateness for
  children, 109

U

unhappiness, 71
unity, 15–27

Scripture Index